Faint Echoes of Laughter
By
Stacey Danson

When I ended my biography, Empty Chairs, I was utterly drained. I had reached a point where the exhaustion of recalling and writing of my early life depleted me so completely that I fell ill.

The guilt of not having kept my promise to Jenny urged me on to complete the book, it weighed heavily on me. I wanted to be free of it.

The fact that so many people, all strangers, care about the what, and the why of the remainder of my life, and by extension those others that peopled my life, has shaken me more than a little. Folks have asked me for more; … some sort of closure by proxy I guess.

The response of readers to "Empty Chairs" caught me by surprise.

The comments for the most part have been incredibly generous.

I have made the decision to write book 2 now and am relieved.

However, I knew that I needed to do one final thing before I could begin.

I had procrastinated for weeks, tossing the idea around and finding too many excuses not to do what needed doing. Finally I was angry at my own inaction…I decided *'what the hell … just go for it'. What harm could it do?*

I have packed in a lot of living in the years since I had walked away from my nightmarish childhood.

I am after all a lot older now; four decades plus in fact, and surely visiting the places of my youth no longer had the power to cause me pain.

I was wrong.

It was not so much the places…it was the memories attached to those places that even now had a power over my emotions.

I made the short trip by bus, and got off well before the stop I needed. I wanted to walk and calm myself before going into *that* neighborhood, before standing in *that* street, before looking at *that* house.

I had expected it to change. Surely, there should be a blazing crucifix on the front lawn, or at the very least a police tape declaring it to be a crime scene. My childhood had been murdered in that house.

I hoped that the bricks and mortar that had encompassed the horrors of my younger years would have been torn down completely; yet there it stood. Newly restored and painted , and by the looks of the restoration the place had been made a National Trust building by the powers that govern the preservation of the gracious old homes of a long gone era.

I'm not certain how long I stood across from my old home; I remained partially hidden behind trees that were probably the only things still living in that street from the years of my youth.

I laughed out loud when I realized I had concealed myself…there was no one alive in this place that could touch me now. Yet I remained concealed, as the shafts of remembered pain and paralyzing fear began tearing their way back into my consciousness.

I hadn't been back, not in all the years since I left on that hot morning in November 1965. I had stopped myself from coming here. What was to be gained by it?

Yet when I decided to write part two of my biography "Empty Chairs", I knew deep in my gut, that I would have to go back and confront the demons. I wouldn't write the book unprepared this time. I knew in advance that I would have flashbacks. I thought I was well prepared and therefore would remain immune to the pain associated with remembering.

I guess I still think of myself as six foot tall and bullet proof, especially when it comes to brazening my way through my crazy life.

It only took a few minutes standing in *that* street, looking at *that* house for me to realize I was wrong, I was never going to lay *all* those demons down. I had never been bullet proof; I simply presented myself that way. I doubt very much that I had fooled many folks that looked beyond the façade I presented.

Most of my demons and their causes had been dealt with…but not this place…never this place. My screams and pleas for mercy and help went unanswered inside those walls. It was here that I forever lost the ability to trust, and learned too early that human beings were capable of inflicting dreadful acts upon their own species.

I stood in that street in 2011 and I felt dizzy and once again fleetingly helpless. My stomach clenched and I felt the sour burn of bile in my mouth.

This had been a mistake.

I took one last look. *She* had died in that house. That was my only thought when I turned and walked away.

As dreadful as it sounds that thought gave me comfort.

I hated myself for feeling that way, yet I have been honest all the way along, no point in now trying to kid myself or anybody else that I had hoped she wouldn't meet a bad end. I wished for it on and off over many years.

She didn't have a bad ending.

In fact, she died the way most folks would wish to go out; she died peacefully in her sleep of old age. Please don't anyone ever tell me again, "What goes around comes around." The day she died proved to me beyond any doubt that that handy little belief was total bullshit. Unless the article in the obituaries was wrong…and why would it be? All the horrific manners of death that I had wished upon her evil soul didn't come to pass. Wishing that she would fry slowly in hell doesn't make me a resoundingly good person…but I have never pretended to be anything other than extremely human.

I hurried back to the bus stop. My determination to cover as much ground as I could today was still intact.

I wanted to do it *all* today…I wanted to prove to myself that I had grown well beyond the untrusting youngster that had first turned to the streets of Sydney for solace in a world gone mad.

The Botanical Gardens were a great place to begin … I had known many moments of happiness there, sleeping in a sandstone overhang on the water's edge. I smiled as I recalled my utter wonder the first night away from the madness, I had found this place and I spent that night lying under a sky filled with stars I had never dreamed existed.

I headed back to it, my instincts taking my feet where they needed to go. I smiled when I saw it, it remained as I remembered it, and blessedly unchanged, no disrespectful graffiti adorned it. The sandstone glistened in the morning sunlight … eons old and unmarked by the 21st century city that hovered on its edges.

I sat on the sandstone allowing the warmth to seep from the rock into my body, drawing peace from it as I had done countless times in those years on the streets. I also recalled the nights I sat in the rain or lay under hedges in the mud to hide from a gang of Skinheads.

The sunshine memories won, hands down.

I walked down the pathway that bordered Sydney Harbor to my favorite fishing spot, and smiled at some young guys trying their luck with a line.

I backtracked and headed deeper into the gardens to a kiosk I once knew well. It had been remodeled but still stood in the same place. I purchased food for the birds and sat on the edge of the lake feeding them and marveling that the stepping-stones out to the island where the birds roosted at night were still there. I wondered how many others had sought safety there at night as I had done, so long ago.

 Funny isn't it, the way we color memories through time, seeking out the glimpses of the happier more brightly tinged moments.

I glimpsed the fear and hunger briefly … and let it go.

I am not afraid and hungry now.

An entire lifetime separated me from the physical harm of the bad stuff. Memories can only cause you pain if you allow them too. Yeah, sure…and a pink pig just flew by my window.

I wandered through the city streets to Hyde Park, to the other fountains that still stood, unrelenting survivors of a time gone by. Unrelenting survivors…

I glimpsed in their crystal water the laughing faces of my friends. I could almost hear the squeals of delight we used to make when taking a weekly bath in the fountains during the summer months. They were good memories. I resolved not to think about the bad stuff, not here, not now, not yet.

I left the beauty of the parks, and made my way down to the docks.

I barely recognized the area we kids had called home. The container terminals were huge now and no visible remnant remained of the area where we had lived in the shipping container we called "The Palace".

What had I expected?

A shrine to the memory of all those wonderful, crazy, half feral kids that had once shared some years of their lives with each other in this place.

There never would be a shrine. Not here.

Their shrine would be in my memory, my thoughts…and if I was fortunate perhaps in the thoughts of some kind folks that would get to know them a little through my words on a page.

I sat quietly for a long while, then took the short walk back to the main street of Sydney and caught my bus home.

I will journey back to the streets of King's Cross some other day. For the moment, I simply wanted to go home.

Home. I am safe. I am happy. I am ready …

So…let's begin the day after Empty Chairs ended.

I don't know how much more I can share, yet I want those of you that cared enough to ask, to at least understand that I am here, I am happy with my life in 2011. I have known love; I have experienced the privilege of motherhood. I have learned that my life has value.

Please understand at the outset, that I cannot possibly recall conversations in absolute detail, what I can recall was what prompted a conversation, and what happened as a result of it. I can recall in detail certain incidents, accidents and events that shine through as important and on reflection, pivotal, in what altered my life, and my perceptions of it. These are the things I can share in the knowledge that they as accurate as I can make them.

Thank you all, for caring enough about this stranger to ask for more…

"Faint Echoes of Laughter." Second Edition.

Chapter 1.

March 1966. Location "The Palace" a damaged shipping container on the docks, in Sydney, Australia.

I wanted everything.

Or at least my almost twelve-year-old version of what everything was.

I wanted a bed, a real mattress, and sheets and blankets. Oh, yeah… that had to be high on my list. Sleeping on concrete with newspaper mattresses is not something I would recommend, but at the time, I was very thankful for it.

I wanted to sleep without clutching my flick-knife.

I wanted to eat fresh untainted food…until I could eat no more.

I wanted to feel safe.

I wanted to laugh and mean it.

I wanted to travel to all the wonderful places I had read about in the library. I wanted to see the magnificent paintings in the Louvre and the Metropolitan Museum of Art in New York.

Most of all at that moment, I wanted Baby Jenny to stop crying…

Jenny cried herself to sleep again last night. I wish she would stop. I wish I didn't have to hear her pain. She lay in the darkness and sobbed. Surrounded by people, yet always alone. The sound pierced what was left of my heart.

She was so small, and so broken.

The knowledge that not one of us could reach out to her and offer her comfort made me angrier, if that were possible. It seemed that anger fuelled many of my days and nights back then.

Being in the same place for three days straight was obviously good. Knowing that the entrance to the "Palace' was guarded by the guys every night had allowed me to relax, not completely, but enough that I was benefitting from a few hours of unbroken sleep.

The bruising on my outer body from the rape was slowly beginning to fade. The bruising to my mind still had a long way to go.

Jamie had mentioned that he would sit down and go over the rules with me today; I was a little edgy about that.

I appear to have an allergy to rules.

But I had already figured that he was probably right; with this many people all trying to get along in a confined space you would need some sort of order.

I wandered outside, wondering how the day would pan out. It was autumn now, and the breeze coming in across the water had a touch of coolness that hadn't been there a few shorts weeks ago. It felt good. The days were still warm with Mother Nature throwing in a few scorching hot ones to remind us that she hadn't settled into an autumn pattern just yet.

I hadn't experienced a winter out here, not yet. The one coming would be the first of many. Sydney winters are reasonably temperate, we don't get snow, and being on the coast meant no frost to speak of, that much I had learned from my regular jaunts to the library.

However, the temperature would be cold to those of us living in the 'Palace'. It could get down as low as 5 and 6 degrees Celsius. Living in a metal container would take a little getting used to; blankets were a rare and highly prized possession. It could and would get dreadfully cold, but I would look back on the alternative and be thankful for where I was now.

I was nervous. Crowds and I were also allergic to each other. I appear to have rather a lot of things that have that affect on me. Some things I would never be comfortable with no matter how often I found myself in the same situation.

To this day I am always edgy and on heightened alert in a crowded place. Yet I can't deal with being confined either. I have dreadful panic attacks if I am caught anywhere small and dark; even knowing where that fear comes from hasn't ceased the attacks.

A small place like 'The Palace" seemed to be overflowing with people, although there were only 15 of us, and except for nightfall many of the residents would be gone for a few hours each day. I was unused to dealing with a group of people.

My preference had always been to be alone as often as I could. I watched a small knot of the girls chatting quietly to each other, one of them made her way over to where I had sat myself.

"Sassy?" The pregnant girl named, 'Momma' for obvious reasons said.

"Uh-huh?"

"We were wonderin'; why are you here, I mean why are you …not at home, you know?"

"Why do you want to know?"

"Why?" she repeated, seeming surprised that I would ask, "Because I guess we're just curious. You know?"

"Oh. Um…look thanks for asking and all, but I'm not up for talking about it."

"We all have reasons to be here, you know." She was clearly offended.

"Hey, sorry, okay. I don't mean to be rude, or anything. But I just don't think it's any ones business but mine. Does it matter?

"I guess not. Well, I'm here 'cause I was too scared to tell my folks I was pregnant." She said and waited for my response.

"What would they have done to you?"

"I dunno. I mean at the time I was scared. Then once I left I didn't feel like I could go back, you know."

"Who was the fa…um…does the father of the baby know?"

"Yeah. He's cool with it, you know. But it's not like he loves me or anythin'."

It would be frightening to be pregnant out here. I figured it would be frightening at any time.

"So…are you scared?"

"Of course not…well not much, you now?" She said.

She seemed uncertain about standing there; she was shifting from foot to foot. "C'mon, I'll show you where the toilets are that are safe to use."

I had already been shown those, but decided it was not gonna break my ass to go with her. They were a fair distance from 'The Palace'. Apparently the dockworkers or wharfies as they were known, seldom needed to come down this far, it was only an area where they dumped damaged containers after all.

"So, does being pregnant feel weird?" I asked.

"Weird? I guess. It's getting really uncomfortable tryin' to sleep on the ground now, I keep wanting to shift around and I run outta room, you know?"

I had no idea of what it would feel like being kicked and punched from the inside, "Does it hurt?"

"Nah, you know. It's sorta nice when he lets me know he's there, you know."

I had begun to figure that 'Momma' ended all her sentences with the words 'you know'. She wasn't actually asking a question.

"So what makes you think it's a he?"

"Dunno, I guess I just didn't wanna keep callin' the baby 'it' all the time, like it was a thing, you know."

I had the fleeting thought that it might actually feel kind of nice to have something like that as a part of who you were; then I thought a little more about it as I looked at her swollen belly, and her pudgy hands and feet. I gave myself a mental shake. Feeding one mouth was hard enough, how the fuck was she going to manage to look out for a tiny little baby.

"Momma, are you gonna keep it … um—him?"

"Well, yeah! Of course. We can all chip in and help, it will be nice, like a family, you know?"

"But…what? Um, yeah, yeah, sure. I get that." The idea of a tiny little baby here in the cold container made me cringe. But if it were loved, I figured that would make all the difference.

I had already spoken more than I normally would. It was none of my damned business what she decided to do, and I knew nothing about baby humans. My reading up at the library hadn't covered anything like that. I made a mental note to look up babies next time I went to the library. I looked at her again and she was patting her stomach…"Do you think the baby can feel that?" I asked in spite of myself.

"I'm not sure, you know. But sometimes when he is kickin' real hard; if I just rub my stomach, it stops, like he knows it's okay, you know?"

"Cool." I didn't know what the hell else to say. "When are you having it … I mean, him?"

"I don't know. I think soon, cause he's gotta be runnin' out of space in here," she said looking down at her protruding gut.

"So how long does it usually take?"

"I'm not real sure, maybe a year."

"Man, that's a long time. Um … I could look it up, at the library I mean."

"What Library?"

"The big place over near that real pretty church on the edge of Hyde Park and the Domain."

"Wow, you can go in there?"

"Yeah, for free. You can read about all sorts of things, and it's got air conditioning, you can sit and read for hours if you want."

"Why would you do that?"

"To learn about stuff…"

"What stuff?"

"I don't know...Just stuff, like where countries are and where we are…all sorts of stuff."

"Oh. Do you think they'd have books about babies?"

"I'm pretty sure they'd have something. It never hurts just to ask."

"When do you go, to the library I mean?"

"Every chance I get. I have so much stuff I want to know. It'll take forever."

"Can you maybe, look at a book about babies and tell me what it says? You know, about having them and stuff?"

"Sure. That's cool. Why don't you come with me?"

"Can you just bring the book back?"

"No. Can't do that, cause I have no fixed address to give 'em. I have to read and look up things while I'm there."

"Well, you look it up and then you can tell me about it, you know. I don't like going anywhere at the moment, in case you know, the baby decides to come."

"Oh… that makes sense. I'll take a look and tell you what I find, how would that be?"

"Good. Um-thanks, Sassy. You know?"

"Yeah. I know."

I have re-read this part with a smile and not a little amazement. I knew how to make a guy orgasm in about two minutes flat, I knew about sadism, and brutality…I knew about cruel dark things that most folks never even imagine.

I knew absolutely nothing about babies and their birth.

The 1950's wasn't an era when these *delicate* issues were discussed. Nothing was printed in magazines, newspapers and any print media that was readily available, and now well into the swinging 1960's the naiveté was causing a mini population explosion as free love met the great uninformed.

I decided to ask some of the others if they knew anything definite about the actual physical act of childbirth. Maybe some of them had younger siblings at home. Then I figured that 'Momma' would already have done that, and besides that would mean I'd have to initiate conversation with strangers

Maybe I'd just ask Jamie. He'd been on watch the night before, and was now catching a few hours sleep at the back of the area that was screened with old blankets for privacy. Whoever was on night watch slept undisturbed there for a few hours after sunrise, in the meantime it looked to me like some general chores were being done.

A couple of the kids nodded to me as a form of hello, I nodded back. I had no idea how to mix with a group of any size, so I watched what they did, and stayed out of the way as much as I could. Jamie would tell me what I needed to do when we talked later.

"Hey, Sassy, could you give me a hand to get some fresh water?" A pretty girl asked the question; I couldn't remember her name.

"Yeah, yeah sure." I stood up and waited to see what she did.

She grabbed a bucket, then another one and handed it over to me. "Momma normally does this, but the buckets gettin' too heavy for her."

"Sure, I understand. Just show me where and tell me how much, okay?"

She gave me a smile. She sure was pretty. I figured her to be around 14 or so.

I followed her outside, remembering where the girls had shown me the taps on my first night here. We walked in silence most of the way then I spoke up, "Um, I can't remember your name."

"It's Cassie. Leastways that's what I call myself here."

"Cool. I'll remember."

"So, Sassy. What do ya think so far, about the place I mean, and us?"

"I don't know yet. It's only been three days. It feels strange."

"Un-huh. Just do your share of the chores, we are all pretty much okay to get along with…sort of, we fight a lot, but there's nothing in it, not really."

"Yeah."

"You don't say much, do you?"

"Nope. I guess I haven't got much to say. Not my place to be sticking my nose in, especially when I don't know how it all works."

"You're smart."

"No…not really. I'm just real careful is all. Except when I'm not, I have a really rotten temper."

She smiled again. We topped the buckets up and carried them back, trying not to spill too much on the way. This was the drinking water. It tasted okay as long as you didn't mind the metallic tang.

Jamie was awake and sitting outside having a smoke when we got back. He nodded and gave us a grin.

Cassie leaned towards me and whispered, "Jamie isn't a happy person in the mornings. It's best to let him have a couple of smokes before talking to him."

I nodded and filed the information into my good things to remember slot. My headspace was getting seriously overcrowded with all these new thoughts.

I sat back down on my sleeping space and started to read it.

Oh, hell…that sounds weird.

We slept on newspapers, collected from everywhere. The thicker the pile the better and it formed a barrier of sorts between our bodies and the metal underneath.

Newspapers were valuable, we slept on them, used them to get a fire started, read them, and wiped our asses on them. It took me a little while to get the in-joke amongst the kids. If someone were feeling grumpy about anything at all they would usually say, "Well, read my ass!" It seemed to diffuse some situations. Although I was to learn that fights were a common occurrence. I had just started reading an article about the Vietnam place that I had learned about at the library, when Jamie called me outside.

"How's it goin', Sass?"

"No complaints so far."

"Good. I noticed you helping Cassie out with the water. You can do that every morning, okay. For two weeks, then we change the chores around."

"Who decides on who does what?"

"I do."

"Just you?"

"Yup, just me. The only thing we all decide together is who gets asked to join, or asked to leave. I still have the last vote if we can't agree."

"So, tell me what can cause someone to be asked to leave? And are they really asked, or are they told?"

"You like words, don't you?"

I laughed. "You noticed."

"Let's get serious, okay? The rules here are simple enough. Everyone pulls their weight. Everyone shares, food, drinks, smokes. It all goes into a central place and at sundown every day we go through it and share it out."

"What about Baby-Jenny? Surely she doesn't have to do too much, she's so tiny?"

"Jenny is the one exception, and at the moment so is "Momma'. Until she's had the baby, she doesn't need to do her chores. She's getting too big and uncomfortable to do too much. Understood?"

"Sure. I get it. Do any of you know anything about having babies? I mean, like when will she have it? And what happens while she's having it?"

"I've never delivered one that's for certain, I know a little from what other people have told me, and two of the girl's parents had a baby before they left home, so they know a little. How hard can it be? Women do it every day?"

"Sure, sure. I'm glad someone knows something about it. But 'Momma' said she thinks it takes around a year for it to be born? That doesn't sort of sound right to me. I might check it out at the library. Momma seems to think it's easy. I hope she's right. Not that it's my business."

"It's all our business, 'cause it affects the group as a whole. Can you go up to the library today, and take a look? I'll come too."

I was surprised at first that he'd said he'd come, then he explained, "You're new to the group, Sass. You might get some good information, but there is no guarantee anyone will listen, 'cause they don't know you yet, and they wouldn't completely trust what you have to say. I'll bring Jenny along. Is there stuff she can look at?"

"Yeah, heaps of great picture books, with baby animals in 'em and, oh, man so much other great stuff she gets to see."

"Good. In about an hour or so, okay?"

"Yeah. Cool."

I have to admit I was thrown. *I* was the one who didn't trust people. I guess I wrapped it around me like a protective shield. It made me pause and think when Jamie said that the others wouldn't trust me yet. I hadn't given their feelings about my presence a great deal of thought. Nothing wrong with my ego…. Lesson learned. One of many I would absorb over the months and years to come.

We arrived at the library soon after opening, and as usual, it was almost empty this hour of the day.

"Hello, Dear." Said the nice lady at the desk.

"Morning, Eunice. Can you tell me where I can find books on babies? Having them and looking after them?"

She glanced at me with concern, and then glared at Jamie. I caught the look and laughed. "No! I'm not, and he isn't. Just want the information for a friend is all."

She didn't look convinced, but walked out from behind her desk and we followed her to the non-fiction books. She suggested that we might like to "freshen up" in the rest rooms before we started reading. Jamie looked at me and then at Jenny. He whispered, "We are freshened up." I cracked up laughing which caused Eunice to glance across with an expression of impatience. We settled down with difficulty. Jenny kept giggling about that for the entire morning. Jamie grinned and said, "Thank fuck she hasn't seen us in winter." He pinched his nose, which set Jenny and I off again. Eunice looked over, but this time she had a tiny smile on her face.

There was a whole shelf and more about babies, and more specifically childbirth. Some of them she had pointed out where written in medical jargon we wouldn't have a hope of understanding, but there were a few others, clearly intended for non-medical readership. Jamie and I grabbed two each and went to sit down, after securing a pile of beautifully illustrated children's books for Jenny to look through.

Jenny was totally engrossed, carefully looking at the illustrations as if committing them to memory.

"Shit! It says here that it takes 40 weeks before the baby is born … that's roughly 10 months. 'Momma' has to have been with us for at least 7 months now, I think. She was a couple of months gone when she arrived. That means she must be gonna have it any time now, according to this." Jamie kept his voice lowered in keeping with the silence signs posted all around the place.

I nodded. I was too caught up trying to understand what I was reading about the womb, and contractions, and the placenta. This was seriously scary stuff.

The information I pointed out to Jamie included details of how close to the baby to cut the umbilical cord, and how important it was to deliver the placenta.

There were sections on breach birth, when the baby came out feet first, and how the cord could become caught around the baby's throat.

We may have gone into the library fairly confident that we could handle anything.

We came out of there scared shitless.

"A little knowledge can be a dangerous thing." I'm never certain about who said that, was it Alexander Pope?

Jamie had gone to the library feeling confident that we as a group could handle the birth of Momma's baby, he'd returned from the library with deep worry lines etched on his forehead.

"We don't wanna spook, Momma. The books told us all the bad stuff that can happen. But most females seem to do it more than once. So how bad could it be?" I said.

Jamie didn't look reassured.

"I never figured it could go wrong. I mean…. No, I just didn't think about it at all." He admitted.

"Well. It's not as if we can shove in a plug and stop it from ever happening. Is it?"

He just looked at me and shook his head. Seemed he was trying not to laugh.

It appears that I occasionally said stuff that he found funny. I was being deadly serious.

But in case I got the idea that he would always laugh at my expressions, he also called me blunt, rude, obnoxious, and a whole lot of other interesting terms in the years that followed. Some I had to look up the meaning of. He helped me expand my vocabulary immensely.

Jenny was even more silent than usual on our way back to the docks. She was perched on Jamie's shoulders like a little frail bird.

I watched her face from time to time. She had a way of shielding her thoughts, as if a blank canvas had been stretched across her pretty features, simply waiting for someone to add color and vibrancy.

She caught me looking and put her head on the side, as if deciding she was comfortable with that or not.

She gave me a half grin, fleeting, but I'd seen it. Then she stuck her tongue out at me and gave me a bigger one.

I laughed out loud.

It was a beginning.

The morning routine was simple, I had no work to go to and I couldn't sing like a couple of the kids that earned a few bucks a day doing that. I fetched the water with Cassie, and then I was on newspaper gathering duty. A couple of us would do the rounds of the parks after lunchtime and gather all the newspapers discarded by the lunch crowds.

We'd then head down to the Railways stations of Town Hall and Wynyard and collect the folded papers from the trashcans. It was a good way of keeping out the cold, including putting layers between your outer clothing and your skin, like a thermal blanket, noisy to sleep on but hell it provided some warmth.

At night, we would put everything in a special spot, food, liquid, smokes, papers and any dollars we had managed to beg…or steal.

Jamie was still working up at the bakery and Mrs. McDowell was our main source of food. I took to going down to the markets early with Cassie to see if we could scrounge some edible fruit and some vegetables that we could throw in the pot over the 44-gallon drum we used for a warming fire and cooking. Plus the markets were coming up on Sunday. I wondered if I'd see Animal again.

Meat was a luxury, we didn't think about it much. We were all being hippies before the term meant anything.

I had been there a week or more when Jamie decided I had better meet 'Big Mike'. Big Mike was in charge of this area of the docks, and he knew we were there and said nothing as long as we didn't make trouble. He had his own reasons for not wanting the cops around.

He and his mates supplied all the wood for our fire, in exchange for having their cars washed once a week. They even popped down occasionally with an old blanket or something we could use.

As soon as I clapped eyes on Big Mike, I understood his name. The man was huge. He wore the navy blue singlet and shorts that the dockworkers lived in, well he kind of wore them. The shorts were struggling a little with the height of the man. He had to be well over 6ft tall, and his hands were huge. He was muscled and didn't look to have an ounce of excess flesh anywhere.

Jamie said that all of them had to meet the guy, not so much for approval…more so that the man would know if strangers were hanging around. It was an act of courtesy. The docks were ruled by this man…on one level. The other level belonged to the suited gentleman we saw about on occasion. The ones I recalled having asked Animal about months before.

I asked Jamie the same question, and I got the same damned answer. "You don't need to know these people, Sassy. Stay out of their way. Understand?"

Sure, I understood. I understood that just fine. I also understood that these guys were loaded for bear. I recognized the tell tale bulge in the suit I had gotten used to seeing whenever Nick's boys would come around to collect the earnings, back at 'Hell Central.' They were sporting shoulder holsters.

Jamie made very certain to get my word that I would stay away from these people.

I gave him my word. That was all he seemed to need.

So, we walked down to the area Big Mike normally had his morning smoko. He was sitting with some mates and they were all talking up a storm.

They called out friendly hellos to Jamie.

"So…you got a name, lass?" The giant asked.

"Yup."

"Weeelll…what is it?"

"Sassy. Or Sass."

"And are you?"

"No I'm the shy one in the bunch."

He laughed as I had hoped he would. "Jamie, Lad. You might have your work cut out for you with this'n I'm thinkin'."

Jamie shook his head…"Tell me about it."

The big man laughed again. I walked over closer and stuck out my hand. He looked surprised but took it in his huge paw and shook it. "Manners yet!"

I grinned and decided for once in my stupid life to keep my mouth shut.

Big Mike lit up a smoke and offered one to Jamie and me. I grabbed it and he threw me some matches. I lit Jamie's and mine and handed the matches back.

You know sometimes I just don't have a choice about what comes out of my mouth…it's like I think it and out it comes…

I grinned up at the big man, "You wanna watch that smokin', Big Mike, wouldn't wanna stunt your growth."

'Sassy!" moaned Jamie grabbing my hand and dragging me away.

I could hear Mike laughing, he called out, "Watch yourself with this one, Jamie. She ain't like the others."

But I was. I was just like the others. Except for the fact that I used my mouth as a barrier and not my fists.

Not yet anyways.

Chapter 2

The days began to take on an aura of comfort, not one of belonging.

I craved that belonging feeling without even being certain what it really was.

I needed to belong. I wanted to feel… what? Safe? Yes, safe that's what it was. I wanted to just be safe. Without being afraid, that something or someone would come along and tear it all to hell.

I didn't see Animal the first week I went back to the markets. His knife stall was there and I asked the young guy about him. He asked who I was and why I was asking. I just said, "No big deal, my names Sassy. Animal and I are sort of friends."

"Oh, so, you're her are you? Bit young for him ain't ya?"

"What? Don't be bloody stupid. It's not like that. He really is my friend."

"Yeah? Whatever you say. I'll tell him you was here when I see him."

"Fine." I was angry, but I guess other people probably thought the same thing. I hoped Animal's missus wasn't one of them.

I hadn't gone back up to the Cross since the rape. I was scared. I had my knife on me and wasn't too sure if I'd pull it or not if I saw one of the bastards that had beaten and raped me and left me for dead.

Animal had warned me months before never to go up against someone who doesn't care if they live or die.

Had I become one of those people?

I wanted to live, just not the way I had lived until now. I needed to hang on to the passionate desire I had to experience a different kind of life. I was struggling on the inside with the occasional thought that it may just be easier to give up. I have no real idea why I never did, not completely anyway. I came closer than I would have believed possible back then.

The anger simmered just below the surface, I covered it well or so I thought.

I caught Jamie watching me with a worried frown sometimes, I would ask him what was wrong, or if I was wearing something that belonged to him. He would just grin at me and shake his head most of the time, although every so often he'd say "Just watchin' you burn, Sass; just watchin' you burn."

I knew what he meant. I wished I could find a way to stop that burning. I have spent a lot of years looking for ways to make it stop. It took me decades to discover that I needed to let go of the anger. It took more years still to do it. But at that time, and in that place I was a walking time bomb ready to blow.

I hadn't seen Paulie since a couple of days after the rape, the beating that went with it had left me immobile for a while.

I wondered if he even gave a damn about what had happened to me. I knew he had been the one to tell the pimp Drew where I was. Carol (one of Drew's ladies) had tried to warn me. I should have taken more heed of what she said, getting over confident had almost gotten me killed.

I wanted to confront Paulie and asked Jamie about it. He said it was up to me, but he wanted to be there when I did.

That made my mind up for me, I wasn't about to drag Jamie into my problem. He had been good to me, and he had a whole lot of people that depended on him being around.

Besides why the hell would Paulie give a crap? I was just some stupid street kid who didn't matter a damn. It would be no skin off his nose if he never saw me again.

Once I recognized the truth in that I decided not to be worried if I saw him or not.

I was more concerned about Drew's thugs. It worried me a lot that they might find out where I was staying and come here and cause trouble for the rest of the group.

Jamie's response to that was almost flippant, "If they come, they come, Sass. Worrying about it won't change it; besides there are a couple of us here that would not like them being here one little bit." That was all he said.

I knew Jamie carried a gun…and so did the 'Flyman'. I wasn't certain if any of the others carried …but I suspected they might. It took me a few months to find out why they carried at all. It didn't concern me, I carried a flick knife myself so it would be pretty stupid to be too curious about them wanting weaponry.

The nights were definitely becoming cooler and the mornings were getting chilly. The fire stayed lit later; and a few of us would sit around listening to the top 40 on the small radio. Batteries were one of our most important must haves, the music was an escape hatch and we were lucky enough to be living in a decade that inspired some of the most amazing stuff ever written.

We sang along … or tried to. My voice was bad … but Cassie and another girl called Kit had fabulous voices, it was a real pleasure listening to them both.

I came to love the compositions of Harry Chapin and Jimmie Webb.

McArthur Park sung by Richard Harris … and Harry Chapin's "All my life's a circle" were my favorites for a time, as was anything by The Beatles and The Rolling Stones.

It was around 9.00 am on a Friday morning when Momma went into labor. Her water broke and she began crying and saying over and over again, "I want my mom."

Jamie sat and talked with her a while, and then he left to get some help. She was getting hysterical and we were all trying to calm her down.

She wouldn't be calmed.

Rightly or wrongly, she wanted her mother. I found that strange back then. I guess my perceptions of motherhood were pretty well negative. I had never once wanted my mother after I walked away from the house of horrors. I recalled wanting her badly when I was very small, she soon took care of that. Some women don't deserve the title of mother. Gwen had been president of that particular club.

Jamie was back in around 20 minutes and Big Mike was with him. Big Mike carried Momma outside and laid her on a pile of rugs that he had spread out on the back seat of his car. Jamie climbed in the passenger seat, after telling us not to worry. He was going to ring Momma's mom from the hospital. She had decided for herself that she wanted her mother more than anything else.

We all mooched around for most of the day. I remember the library books said that first birth could take a very long time.

By midnight, we were all pretty worried, and couldn't do much except reassure each other that she was in hospital and Jamie was there, so she'd be fine.

Baby Jenny was always anxious when Jamie wasn't around, I don't remember hearing her speak at all that day. Change unsettled the little one. I knew her for a lifetime and it always remained that way. She would settle for the bad in life simply because it was familiar. How incredibly sad and yet understandable that was.

It was around 3.00 am when we heard the car, and we all went outside to meet them. Big Mike gave Jamie a bear hug, then he got back in his car and left.

We pounced on Jamie for news, all at once.

He looked weary, but happy. "Momma had a little girl. She had some problems so they had to do an emergency Caesarian, but she'll be fine; and her mother is with her."

Everyone started talking at once. When Jamie had settled down, relit the fire, and had a cigarette he explained that Momma had come from a small country town around six hours drive away.

He smiled as he told us that her mother had screamed, laughed, and cried all at once when Jamie rang her, she was so flustered she had to put her husband on the phone. He had cried as well. They had been searching for Elizabeth (Momma's real name) ever since she disappeared. They had even had private detectives looking for her.

They drove straight from the country to the city hospital and arrived in time to see their daughter just before she was taken to surgery.

Jamie said that Big Mike had been great; he had spoken to Momma's folks for a long time while they all waited.

Whatever he had said Jamie was thankful for it. Momma's folks asked a lot of questions but weren't angry once they realized that Jamie wasn't the father of the baby. They thanked him for looking out for her for so long, and for contacting them when he knew how to.

It was nice to hear that things were going to work out well for Momma. How sad that the fear of confiding in her folks had kept her out here all that time.

Her parents sounded like good people according to Jamie. He was shaken by what had happened though. We all talked about what might have happened to Momma and her baby if she hadn't wanted to be with her Mother.

Jamie said that the emergency surgery had happened because she had started to hemorrhage. She and the little one could have both died had she had the baby in 'The Palace' as she had planned to do.

We were all quiet the next day. What could have happened to Momma badly shook the belief that we as a group could handle anything that came up.

Chapter 3

I wish I could remember the names of all the kids that were in the Palace in those winter days of 1966. But as with any group, things changed quickly and I wasn't on chatting terms with some of the people that seemed to come and go so rapidly.

There was an unwritten law that we all seemed to stick too. If a newcomer stayed for 3 months, they were accepted totally, if they didn't last that long it was "Hi how are you, fit in or leave, and see you around."

I was feeling unwell again, and the pain that had doubled me over in the months before the "Palace" hit me again with no warning. I was with Cassie at Paddy's Markets doing our early Friday morning food gathering, when it hit.

I felt the hot sweat break out and I threw up, then I buckled at the knees as the pain knotted my insides.

Cassie freaked out; she had no idea what to do to help me. I tried to keep walking and couldn't. She half carried, half dragged me outside and was in tears trying her damndest to get me mobile.

"Cassie. Get me some water, love. I'll be okay in a little while." I wasn't sure she'd heard me.

I knew from experience that this was going to be bad. I needed to lie down and curl around myself like a ball till I rode it out.

I vaguely remember what followed, I knew only that my insides felt like they were tearing apart and burning like a fire. I recall being lifted and then I blacked out.

When I came around, I was lying on my sleeping place back in the Palace; sweating badly even though the temperature in the metal container was almost freezing. Someone was holding a bottle to my mouth, an old coke bottle filled with water I think it was. I drank it rapidly and threw it up just as fast.

Then I mercifully blacked out again.

The others told me afterwards that I had been like that for at least 3 days; all they could do was keep giving me sips of water every time I came around.

On day four I woke feeling like a horse had kicked me in the guts. Jenny was sitting next to me, and ran outside calling for Jamie when she realized I was fully awake.

Jamie came in and sat on his haunches next to me. "Fuck, Sassy. Fuck! What the hell was that? Can you understand me?"

His face was pale.

"Sorry. Sorry. I didn't know it would happen again. Sorry. Can I have some water?"

He went to stand up, but Jenny spoke out, "I'll get it."

Jamie put his hand on my forehead. "Thank fuck, you were burning up real bad, Sass. Every time I tried to get you to go to the Hospital you started screaming like the devil was after you."

"Sorry, Jamie. No hospital. Please. I'll be okay now. It just takes a few days and it stops all by itself. I'll be a little shaky but I'll be fine soon. Please no hospitals!"

He could see I was getting upset by the thought of being taken to a hospital, I feel so sorry for what I put him through with that. He was worried sick, and I certainly didn't help by screaming to be left alone while I was out of it.

Jenny came back with some fresh water and some fruit. Jamie took it and held the bottle to my mouth; I was so dry I emptied it fast. I wasn't up to the fruit, not yet. Just water and lots of it for a day or so, if this thing ran its usual course. The damned pain seemed to be getting worse each time it hit, I was afraid and weakened.

"Just sleep now, Sass. You're safe, I promise. No hospitals. Okay."

Jenny had been back outside and came over to where I was laying; she covered me up with something. I gave her little hand a squeeze, "Thanks, Baby. Thanks."

"She's been sitting next to you for the best part of two days, Sass." Jamie said with a note of pride.

I looked sleepily up into that dear little face and tried to give her a smile. I squeezed her hand again and she gave me a grin. Then I slept.

It took roughly 3 or 4 days for me to feel up to doing much moving around. I sat outside near the fire for a few hours during the day. I drank huge amounts of water and ate boiled vegetables as often as I could stomach them. None of us had any way of knowing that this was the best possible diet I could be on. It was simply all we had.

Jenny had taken to being my watchdog. Bless her dear little heart. She almost snarled like a brave puppy if she thought someone was annoying me…she didn't sound like a young puppy though, "Piss off, and let her rest." That was pretty much all she said.

Jamie was gone 3 days a week working up at the bakery. When he was around Jenny was his shadow, when he was gone, she hung around me like a second skin. Somehow my being ill had made her feel like she was needed. Which indeed she was. Jenny was to spend the remainder of her life needing to feel needed more than any other emotion. It caused her a great deal of pain she didn't ever deserve to feel.

Chapter 4

My health improved fairly quickly and I was back on my feet within a week. Winter had well and truly arrived and I was surprised that I had forgotten my birthday back in April. I had turned twelve. It was now late August.

I had passed the 3 months probation stage.

We added four new members to the group in early spring. Two of them became friends of mine, along with Cassie, Flyman, Baby Jenny, and of course Jamie. Their names were Kirsty and Tilly I'm guessing they were aged around 16. They had both being turning tricks up at the Cross. Both of them decided that they just couldn't keep doing that indefinitely.

Their pimp wasn't happy, and staying up at the Cross had become a very unhealthy place for them to be.

Tilly (Matilda) was a lovely looking girl; she had almost waist length dark hair and a smile that could turn men into puddles. She was a quiet girl, and only spoke if she felt it absolutely necessary.

Kirsty on the other hand was a loud and larger than life redhead, she was always flustered about something, and ready to fight at the slightest provocation. Underneath that bluff and bluster was a tender heart easily damaged.

We didn't use the word 'gay' back then. Gay still meant happy and lighthearted. Tilly and Kirsty were lesbians. Anyone that dared call them dykes had an entire shipping container full of people to contend with.

They were a couple, and that fact tested Jamie's rule about no relationships in the Palace. The girls made a deal not to be overtly physical in front of the rest of us. It was forbidden for the heterosexuals in our group to do so and Jamie applied the rule to everyone. They weren't happy about it, but recognized that the Palace offered them shelter and relative safety; that being so they kept their complaints to themselves.

Feminine Hygiene products were as rare as hen's teeth and expensive to buy. Most people wouldn't give a thought to that, but it was high priority to a bunch of young menstruating females all living in the same place at the same time.

Poor Jamie and the boys joked that they needed to wave a white flag before entering the Palace on any given day in any given month for fear of getting their heads snapped off, or worse yet having some premenstrual female cry all over them. Poor bastards. It couldn't have been any fun at all. Tsk, tsk… Pity.

We girls had a rough roster system worked out. We'd each try and pinch a small packet of tampons every week, so we had a stockpile. Never the same place by the same girl in the same week. It was dishonest, sure it was. But we needed the product more than we needed a gold star on our references for heaven.

As a rule, none of us made trouble by stealing anything that wasn't urgently needed.

I guess it depended on what you considered urgent.

Chapter 5

Quite a few people have asked me over time what caused the other kids in the Palace to be living on the streets.

What was their story?

I have deliberated a long time about just what to tell you the reader here, and it's a difficult situation. I want to help you understand the *Why* of it…for it seems that some folks who have never felt the soul-destroying fear of abuse in any form have a very real problem empathizing with those that have run from it.

We all had reasons.

Reasons—not excuses. There is a huge difference in my opinion.

Sure–some of the people out there on the street had less reason than others, but, the streets were not softer to sleep on or easier to deal with if you had more or less reason to find yourself there.

The streets are an egalitarian place. Everyone on them for whatever reason has the same hard choices to make.

The predators were no less vicious if your reasons were stronger.

We humans can be such a cruel, judgmental species.

The pecking order on the streets—any streets–in any damned country–is simple—only the most vicious in the food chain survive at a visible level.

Only those clever enough to manipulate, and use a weaker beings fears against themselves remain untouched.

Only those that have lost all traces of the humane aspect of being human; those for whom, caring, kindness, pity and love have become unknown words attached to long dead feelings.

Only they become safely visible.

Even those living on the scraps of human remains— the pimps and the pushers, even they have a higher power further advanced by deed in the food chain.

Living on the streets—sure—you may survive it. To do it alone, with no back up, and sustain your humanity— not a snowballs chance in hell.

Being alone sets you apart—instantly. Make no mistake—the predators single you out, and wait. They wait–certain of the fact that, fear, hunger, or one of a countless number of possible addictions—will drive you as part of an unwilling herd to the differing degrees of slaughter of the soul.

Some street dwellers fall into the visibly crazy category.

Who would dare in all conscience put that label on anyone out there, without looking at their own shaky versions of sanity first?

Not I.

The sad folk who were labeled as such attracted attention. Their need was so obvious, it shone like a beacon to the few organizations charged with rescuing those who had slipped through the tears in the fabric of society.

The obviously crazy people tended to survive far better than those of us that still walked the razors edge of what did and did not constitute visibly insane.

I lived on those streets. How the hell I survived those early months alone I do not even begin to know.

What I do know is this. I would not have made it to age twelve, without taking my own life. Or having a lifestyle forced upon me that would ensure I continued to breath whilst dead anyway.

I would not, could not, have survived it alone.

I had reached the end of my endurance. I was filthy dirty, hungry and without hope. I had witnessed too much of the darkness in the human soul. I wanted to just give up. Finish it.

I wanted with everything that was in me to no longer be paralyzed with fear. All I wanted was to feel safe…not rich, successful, beautiful or famous…just safe.

I would have taken my own life, without further hesitation, or thought. Except for this bunch of badly damaged, half-crazy–half-feral street kids. That's what they were, not saints or angels sent from heaven. They were just like me—only they had each other for support.

They saved me, from–me. I have tended to gloss over the negative and focus on the positive. I have always done that, and will no doubt continue to do so. Dwelling on the bad things is not good for my peace of mind.

However, please make no mistake; I was not a young female version of "Huck Finn" setting off on some wonderful adventure.

I was just a kid with a dreadful past. A twelve-year-old girl who wanted so very badly to have a less than dreadful future.

I was fallible, very human and terribly afraid. I was also wary, untrusting—and very, very, angry.

I had never known a childhood. It was ripped away. It was torn apart–together with every fragment of innocence a child has. I was an old woman in a child's body. Searching for the child I should have been, everyplace I went.

The fact that I survived all of it, reasonably sane—and still able to laugh—was not due only to my strength. I don't deny I am strong. I don't deny that I grow weary at times of needing to be that way.

No, I did not survive only through my strength of will. I had no miracle to perform. I survived because I got lucky.

I was taken in to the 'palace' only because one of the kids had chosen to end her struggle with life. She died and left room for one more in their group.

Only one.

Why did they choose me? What complex issues did they discuss that caused me to be selected from the many, many, kids out there?

They chose me simply because they liked my street-name, 'Sassy.' Jamie decided if I had managed to earn a name like that, then I might just be able to make it.

There were no second chances.

This is written with love. They taught me how to feel it.

I need to honor them.

Only three of the group that I owe my own life to, only three, died of natural causes.

Over the next four decades, ten people—ten wonderful, valiant people, ended their own lives. Or they got caught up in a style of life that caused it to be taken from them.

My memories are of them.

My heart aches for all the young ones that will spend another night on the streets of every city and every country.

I am asking each of you that may be reading this to please reach out if you can.

Spend a moment with your own families, and think what it would be like for any one of them to be alone and afraid. Spare a moment to think of all the lonely people who have no friends—no family, and no hope.

Try and allow the thoughts in, no matter how ugly they are. If you can.

A smile from a total stranger can be all it takes to lighten the sadness and renew the hope.

I'm smiling, at the memories and the craziness of the time I spent with them. Every day since those wonderful damaged young street kids entered my life is worthy of remembering.

They allowed me to feel connected to something for the first time in my life.

They dealt with my anger, for it matched their own.

We fought each other fiercely…but mostly we allied against anyone or anything that threatened harm to the unified bunch that we eventually became.

No one is alone, while ever someone cares enough to think of them.

I think of them now as I write this.

Chapter 6

The winter turned to spring and summer was fast approaching.

The seasons becoming melded until, they merged.

Life in the Palace wasn't always smooth sailing.

There were jealousies and spitefulness, hatred and confusion.

Jamie did his damndest to see to it that any person who had a problem with another within the group handled it one on one.

He fought fiercely to prevent small groups fighting one another.

It simply wasn't possible to do that all the time.

So there were flare-ups and fights, no matter how he tried to enforce the rules. A group of volatile and angry young people living in such close proximity had to vent it in some manner.

It was difficult, if not impossible, to stay secluded from that sort of anger.

No matter what my intentions, there were times when I deemed it necessary to make choices about who I supported. I couldn't step back when I felt something was wrong.

Jamie had made one hard and fast rule that he insisted was kept above all others … no sexual relationships within the Palace.

I didn't have a problem with that at all. My body was not about to be joined at the genitals by anyone ever again. Such was my naiveté at age 12.

It wasn't as easy for some of the kids.

Inappropriate sexual behavior is a very common side effect of sexual abuse.

Some of the gang suffered from it, without being able to see why they did what they did. It took me years to understand it myself when I witnessed it as often as I did.

It's simple really, I guess. The abuse itself becomes the way that some young people equate to love.

Touch and physical contact becomes as necessary as breathing, it means they are accepted and cared for if sex is shared. Promiscuity is a common side effect for both sexes.

The most heated arguments seemed to arise from this in particular.

Chapter 7

Christmas was barely a week or so away, and the mood wasn't good.

Christmas out here meant different things to each of us I guess.

My memories of Christmas's past were all bad. Even last year when I'd been on the streets alone for barely a month had bad stuff attached to it, yet it hadn't been nearly as bad as the ones I had lived with back in 'hell central"

I asked Jenny to come for a walk with me down to see Big Mike. I wanted to ask him if he could scrounge up some left over decorations to put up in the palace to lighten the mood up a little.

He gave me a thoughtful nod, and said he'd "see what he could do."

He spoke to Jenny…"I swear you get prettier every day, Jenny. Don't let Sassy here teach you any bad habits."

Jenny grinned at him too shy to respond.

I kept my mouth shut except for a "Gee thanks…Big Mike"

He smiled and wandered off, and we headed back up to the palace. We spent a lot of time outdoors during the heat of the summer. The cooler breezes from the water were good. The heat inside our metal home was dreadful.

When a week had passed and we hadn't seen Big Mike we figured that he had forgotten. It was disappointing; but he didn't owe us anything; and after all he had helped us out with Momma and other stuff like wood for the fire in winter, so we didn't really expect the decorations we just hoped for them.

Jenny was extra quiet. I wondered if she would ever be able to talk about why she was here. I didn't ask her. I hadn't discussed my background with any of them, even Jamie. So I understood that it was not open for general information.

Christmas Eve dawned fiery red. It was going to be a very, very, hot day according to the radio forecasts, with a cool southerly change expected later in the evening.

We all headed up to Hyde Park very early and took a Christmas bath. At least the palace wouldn't stink so badly for Christmas.

It was tempting to just jump in the ocean so close to the Palace, but Mike had warned us all about the sharks, so we didn't dare.

Sydney Harbor wasn't the safest place to swim. We planned on heading down to the Botanical Gardens for a swim in the lake that evening. We figured there wouldn't be many people around because it was Christmas Eve.

The sky began to look dark and threatening early in the afternoon. The southerly buster was heading up the coast rapidly. We were all unusually quiet and sitting around outside in the shade of the container when we heard the sound of vehicles heading toward the Palace.

We headed around the front to see who had arrived and watched in stunned amazement as Big Mike and two of the other guys whose names I can't recall, began unloading boxes of stuff from their cars and placing it in the shaded opening of our tin home.

Big Mike looked uncomfortable; if possible, he was even gruffer than usual. "You lot need feeding up, so we brought you some stuff."

We were all too stunned to say much at all, these hard men were all smiling and a little red faced. I swear if they could have, that they would have scuffed their shoes in the dirt like little kids with embarrassment.

Big Mike shook Jamie's hand and accepted the thank you from him.

I was speechless which wasn't a common occurrence, I just grinned like mad and gave the guys a hurried "Thanks."

They were the unlikeliest Angels you would ever see, sweaty and dirty after a long hot day's work, the sight of them unloading the Christmas goodies and punching one another in the arm in a gesture common amongst males remains etched starkly in my memory.

Big Mike reached into the front seat of his car, and pulled out a parcel that was wrapped up in Christmas paper, with bright ribbons attached. He walked over and handed it to Baby Jenny.

She looked confused and wasn't sure what to do with it.

"The women picked this out for ya, little one." Big Mike said.

Jenny still wasn't sure what to do.

"Go ahead and open it, Jenny." Jamie said.

"Um, later. Later. Okay?" she replied looking very unsure of herself.

She looked at the men, and gave them one of her sweet smiles, "Don't matter what it is. I never had a present before, so...Um...Yeah, thanks, thanks a lot."

The men seemed to understand that she needed to be alone when she opened it.

As for the rest of us, we tore into those presents and boxes like there was no tomorrow…squealing in delighted surprise with everything we found.

There was more food than any of us had ever seen.

 Tinned Hams, fresh pineapples, cherries and plums. Cooked Turkey and Cranberry sauce …with all the trimmings. Fifteen red t-shirts all large sizes. Paper plates, and plastic knives and forks, a can-opener. A Cooler packed with ice, a radio and spare batteries. A big crate of beer and bottles of Coke.

That night, we all huddled around the new radio; it was bigger and put out a better sound than the small transistor we had been using, we sat drinking the beer and singing our version of Christmas carols, none of them repeatable. Trust me.

Jenny sat on her sleeping place; she was a little tipsy as well having been allowed one-half of a small bottle of beer. We glanced at her as she picked up her present and watched the look on her face as she unwrapped it.

It was a baby doll, all soft and dressed in bonnet and booties with a pretty pink knitted dress. "Just what we needed, another fuckin' mouth to feed." she said…but the smile on her face could have lit up the entire city.

We were fed, content, and a little overwhelmed and unsure at the kindness of these people.

Typically, we questioned the motive behind it. We all wanted to believe that maybe, just maybe, they had done it for no motive other than the wish to make this Christmas a good place for us to be. It was an alien experience but a welcome one.

We had only sampled a little of the huge amount of food, deciding to save the rest for Christmas Day

That night we were all tipsy. Strangely quiet as we bedded down for the night. I think we were all a little overwhelmed by the generosity of these men.

It was around 2.00 am Christmas morning I guess when I felt something was wrong. Whatever the something was, it wouldn't let me sleep. I couldn't place it immediately. It was a strange sense of something missing, and it troubled me.

Jamie was on watch; I climbed over the others and hunkered down next to him. Jamie smiled at me and said, "You too hey, Sassy?"

"Yeah, I guess--what is it? Something's different."

We sat a while just listening. Then Jamie said, "Oh shit! It's Jenny, she's not crying!"

My heart was in my mouth. Jamie grabbed the torch and we played it across the others, several of them were already awake, and wondering what the hell was happening.

Jenny lay on her side, sound asleep with both arms wrapped around that doll so tight there was no space between them.

That was the first time I had cried in a very, very, long time. I glanced at the others, without exception we were all affected the same way. No one wanted to look at anyone else, shit we were supposed to be the toughest kids on the block! Hell, we were the only kids on the block. That Christmas was the first real day of Jenny's childhood. From then on, Christmas became Jenny's birthday.

I'd like to tell you that a miraculous change came over her.

I'd like to tell you that she ran around all warm and fuzzy singing songs from 'The Sound of Music.'

I can't tell you any of that, because this is the real world.

That is not what happened.

What did happen was sneaking and slow, almost impossible to see at first.

The changes were far more apparent in the rest of us. If possible, the boys became even more protective. Some of the girls liked it. I resented it like hell.

I resented the implication that as I was a female, and in consequence of not having been born with balls, I had to live by their rules.

The guys were not at all sure if I was going to hug 'em or slug 'em. So distance was kept. Me being me, had already worked that one out way ahead of time.

Keep them guessing. It worked well, for a time.

The days and nights were not all sunshine and roses. Yet compared to what we had all escaped from, 'The Palace' was pretty damn good.

The changes in Jenny became more visible over that summer. She laughed out loud, often. She still didn't like to be touched, but didn't recoil quite as much if you sat too close to her. She had named the doll Francine.

Francine went everywhere with her. If we wanted to sleep without one eye open, we treated that doll with respect.

Jenny began to talk more. At first, it was just asking stuff, regular questions, like, um "What's for food tonight? Can we afford to get some Coke?"

After a time I noticed Jenny trying to make sense out of one of the newspapers we used to sleep on. It hadn't occurred to me that she didn't know how to read.

I had left school after only attending for 3 years; so I was no genius at it, but I knew enough to help her sound out words; the rest of us made time to help her with the alphabet.

Jamie went to the newsagent's shop and offered to work in

back, in exchange for some pencils and crayons and kid's books. The owner of the shop was cool. He let Jamie keep his pride by doing a little tidy up every Saturday. In return, Jenny had a supply of papers, crayons, books, and letters of the alphabet.

She had me writing stories for her that she would read aloud to her captive audience. I always wrote of her as the victor in every situation. She was strong, invincible and needed to be the rescuer and not the rescued. She loved those stories, and throughout four decades, she would mention them every time we caught up with each other.

.Chapter 8

A few weeks later another of the group left. He had only been with us a few weeks and I can't recall his name. That left an opening for one more.

Jamie asked another person to share the Palace. We had all voted and she was accepted by a very small majority, with Jamie needing to cast his vote to have her become a member of the group.

Her name was Juniper … what the hell sort of name was that? Apart from a song, that Donovan sang I had never heard it.

The street girls were normally our eyes and ears. If they spotted a likely candidate worthy of living in "The Palace", the street girls made sure we got a message.

Juniper wasn't recommended by the girls. She came to us on her own.

Most of the run-aways in our experience were just kids who didn't like the boredom of their home life. They were the thrill-seekers. We had no space or patience for that bunch. We called them the 'Circus Freaks'.

The street girls were usually acute judges of who was bored and who was hurting. We never referred to the girls as hookers or whores. They deserved our respect and that's exactly what they got.

Anyone that disrespected the girls, by extension disrespected us. We had earned a reputation on the streets for not taking kindly to anyone who was found guilty of that particular crime.

Judgmental? Hell, yes! We felt we had earned that right, and were naive enough to believe we had the right to uphold it.

I guess Juniper fancied herself as a flower child.

She'd heard we had the market cornered for flower children, she had heard that we were pacifists, who believed in free love. Shit! Free love my skinny-ass, ain't no such animal.

As for being pacifists … sure we were! As long as nobody threatened any one of us.

The boys seemed taken with her. Testosterone tended to get in the way of sense in my way of thinking.

To be fair she had big tits and huge blue eyes or vice-versa. I was probably jealous as all hell. At the time, I thought it was just intuition that told me she was trouble with a capital T.

Jenny hated her from day one. She confided in me that Juniper scared her.

Jenny began hanging around me even closer from the day 'Juniper' arrived. I liked the feeling of her trusting me to look out for her. I liked it a lot.

I watched Juniper like a hawk. So much so, that she complained to Jamie that I didn't like her.

That was her first mistake. Jamie told her in everyone's hearing if she had a problem with me; too damn well tell me about it, and not anyone else stupid enough to listen.

Phew! Man, that felt good. I sat there and watched her squirm. Jenny got a fit of the giggles, and ended up with her head in my lap cackling like a chicken. That distracted me and everybody else. I didn't touch her in response, I was afraid to change the moment. Jenny still didn't like to be touched. We all figured that was never going to change. So the fact that she'd put her head in my lap startled everyone…except Juniper cause she hadn't been with us long enough to understand Jenny's behavior.

Jamie looked at me with a huge grin on his face. I recognized it as pride.

Jenny finished laying her egg, and started up with the hic-ups, which set her off again. The laughter was contagious and we all caught it.

Juniper was clearly not impressed. She said nothing, not then.

When the laughter settled I half-expected Jenny to be embarrassed and move away, she didn't. Jenny sat up and snuggled in under my arm. I was so shaken I didn't know how to respond to her. She took care of that by picking my arm up and draping it around her shoulders. I swear she sat there glaring at Juniper with a look on her little face that clearly said, "Ok bitch, *and now* say something!"

Juniper was clearly humiliated. I felt smug, the bitch had

earned it.

Two days later I was in taking a dip in the fountain with a couple of the others, it was reasonably early in the morning and a Sunday. Hyde Park wouldn't get busy for at least two hours yet.

Jamie and the other boys were a fair distance away lying out under the trees drying off. We weren't stupid enough to swim bare-assed; at least not in daylight hours. So the drying off ritual included a various assortment of clothes.

Summer was our cleanest time.

Jenny as always, wasn't too far away from me; she'd saved some bread scraps and was feeding the pigeons, she laughed out loud at their antics. It gave her pleasure, and made the rest of us smile.

I heard her scream, and turned in time to see Juniper throw Jenny's doll in the dirt and slap Jenny viciously across the face.

I don't remember getting out of the fountain, or running. Jamie was almost there at the same time I was, only not quite soon enough.

I do remember grabbing that bitch by her hair, and slamming her to the ground.

I do remember punching her over and over again.

I don't know what would have happened if Jamie hadn't

pulled me off.

She was pretty messed up. My right hand was bleeding and swelling rapidly.

Jenny sat quietly … too quietly. I walked over to her slowly, terrified that she had broken and retreated back inside her safe place. She looked up at me and put her arms up; the way a baby does when it wants a hug. I picked her up and cradled that baby, and rocked her in that ageless rhythm that must be part of female genetic makeup. We both cried. Jamie offered to carry her back home, I refused. By the time we got back to 'The Palace,' Jenny was asleep. Jamie took her from my arms and lay her down on her sleeping space.

Then I sat watching her anxiously.

I finally felt calm enough to attempt sleep myself.

The pain in my hand woke me.

Jamie dragged me down to see Big Mike. We ended up in the first-aid room…Mike asked the nurse to take a look at my hand after muttering something about "Bloody females."

The nurse bathed it and strapped it. She said I needed X-rays, but she was fairly certain it was broken. She gave me Aspirins and a few for later and insisted I needed a doctor to see it and plaster it properly.

I guess you can figure my response to that.

I'll always be thankful that I didn't take my flick-knife with me on bath days.

Juniper, would be grateful too, if she'd known.

She didn't return to the Palace.

Jenny turned a corner that day. She recognized for the first time in her young life that people cared about her enough to bleed for her if necessary. It changed her. She became a little more adventurous, more confident somehow.

Not hugely so, but enough that she was able to ask and sometimes insist on her own way. Like I said not huge, but a damn good beginning.

I'd always wondered what it would be like to have a sister, Jenny became that, and in some ways, she became my child as well, even though I was only older by four years.

Chapter 9

I finally managed to find Animal at the markets around late summer. He was pleased and surprised to see me.

"Well, Sassy girl, no need to ask if you're doin' okay is there?" He said and gave me a quick hug. I squirmed with discomfort at the unexpected body contact.

"So," he said, "Word on the street is you're living with the bunch down on the docks. Smart move, Sassy. Jamie is good people."

"Yes; he is that. Where the hell have you been, man? I've been down here a lot trying to find you. I even went up to the 'Texas Tavern' a few times but the guys said you hadn't been around in a while."

"Yeah...I took a little holiday with the old lady. We went up to the Great Barrier Reef. You ought to go there one day, Sassy. It's just beautiful."

"Yeah, I read about it at the library...it sounds really cool."

He smiled widely "Yeah...It's that all right."

"Well I'm glad you're in one piece. I was worried."

"Look at the size of ya...worried about me. You are one weird chick."

"Yeah, I know."

"Still got a cocky mouth though, eh?"

"Who me? Nyah…I'm quiet as a mouse. I never got a chance to thank you, for putting that money in my bag, after the rape. It meant a lot to me."

"No need, I felt bad about not bein' able to do more, kid."

"You did more than anyone else ever did, Animal."

"Right. Good. You'll have me crying in me fuckin' beer in a minute."

"Shit! You have beer? Yes please."

He laughed and pulled a bottle out of the cooler.

"Here you go. So how are things down on the docks?"

"Fine. Like you said, Jamie is good people, and we kinda look out for each other. You know the deal."

"How many of you are there now?"

I did a quick tally in my head. "Um…counting me, we have 13 at the moment, we have room for two more, but Jamie's being extra careful cause we had some problems a couple of months back with one of the "Circus Freaks."

"So, Drew's boys give you any more trouble?"

"How the fuck did you find out who raped me? I haven't told anyone who it was."

"Keep your shirt on, Sassy. You know there are no secrets out here. Carol was worried about ya. She asked me if I'd seen ya, and asked me to let her know if I found out where you were. Drew's her pimp…she found out. Nuff said."

"She's a nice person."

"Yeah she is that. So… have you had any more trouble from them?"

"No, none. I haven't gone back up to the Cross-, except to try and find you at the pub. I've figured it was better if I stayed away."

"That's the smart girl I remember. Stay away, okay?"

"Yeah. It's hard though, you know. I wanted to go and cut their balls off."

"I get that. I do. But you'd end up dead, Sassy. Use ya brains. Besides, I hear that they aren't working for Drew no more. Don't ask me where they went. I won't tell ya. Just keep on keeping away from the Cross-. And Sassy…stay away from Paulie as well. Ya hearin' me? Paulie is a piece of shit."

I mumbled something…

"Promise me, kid. Stay away from the place…and especially Paulie. Things have a way of sneakin' up on a person, unexpected like. Maybe somethin' nasty will sneak up on him one day."

"If I believed in God I'd say a prayer for that to happen."

He grinned at me. "You haven't changed a bit."

But I had.

Chapter 10

The years began ticking over and our lives in the palace took on a sense of normalcy.

That was the danger of it.

I began to believe that this life was acceptable; I began to lose sight of my dreams.

After all, I ate on a semi-regular basis, I had a roof such as it was over my head, I had people around me who cared about me, and whom I cared about…perhaps this was as good as it would ever get.

I watched Jenny growing and listened to her interpretation of the future.

That is what on reflection was the catalyst for me. To hear Jenny say with such belief that she was almost big enough to start sitting guard duty at night, as if it were a treasured dream.

She was almost twelve-years-old…going on one hundred. This life was all she had she said…it was all she needed she said.

I took a long hard look at this little world we survived in … and rediscovered my need for more.

It had been all too easy to succumb to the thought that this life was better than 'hell central', and perhaps it was all I needed and deserved.

I was almost sixteen-years-old, and I wanted more, much more.

I began thinking of ways to leave the safety of the palace. I began to get restless and edgy. My gut kept telling me it was time to go. I needed to find a place to go to.

I found myself watching people on their way to whatever jobs kept them in the city for eight hours a day.

The shop girls wore black skirts and white blouses and they worked hard standing on their feet all day. I thought about dealing with people all day who were busy, grumpy and unhappy that they needed to shop at all. I thought about what I'd be tempted to do to the first person that complained at me … and decided that was not what I wanted to do.

The office workers seemed to be a different breed. I watched women hurrying past, dressed in business clothes and business hairstyles. I envied that certain look they wore, that barrier look that said, "I have a busy life."

I began to wonder just what a person had to do to be able to wear that look.

There were no books in the library that would cover that topic … but Eunice the Librarian would know what needed to be learned. I was positive she would, after all, she was a Librarian; back then, that was as close as it got to being a supreme being in my eyes.

I headed up to the Library early; and stood waiting outside for it to open.

Eunice was clearly surprised to see me.

"Well, Sassy…and how are you? I haven't seen you in quite a while."

I could have flipped off a smart assed comment, but this wasn't the place or time for that.

"Mornin', Eunice. I've been kinda busy."

"I'm pleased to see you." she said with a smile. "What are you planning on researching today?"

I liked the way she talked to me, as if I were important. "Researching" made what I did seem relevant somehow.

"Eunice, I want to know what I need to learn to work in an office." I said.

She looked a little taken aback, but indulged me with a smile. "That would depend on what manner of office you worked in, Sassy."

"Aren't they all the same?"

"Oh, no dear. Certainly not. Although some basic principles apply across all the choices." She hesitated as if she were looking for the right words to say; "Most offices would require a minimum level of education, Sassy dear."

"Education? Oh, I see. Schooling…. Thanks, Eunice." I turned and began to walk away when she called me back.

"There are things you could do, that may be all you need to get a job as an office junior, Sassy."

"Like what?"

"Well, most juniors in most offices are responsible for the filing of documents, letters and the like."

"Filing?"

"The alphabetic or numeric way to keep track of all the paperwork an office generates, dear. You read a great deal…you must have noticed how the books appear on the shelves, in sections for the type of book, and then by Author name, strictly alphabetically."

"I hadn't paid much attention to that. So alphabetically, that's the last name or the first?"

"Surname, Sassy. Then strictly alphabetical within that framework."

I must have looked as confused as I felt.

"I don't have time at the moment to show you dear. Go and take a walk around the popular fiction section. I suggest you look in Romance fiction.

"Look for books by Barbara Cartland. Then, look either side of her series and you will see what I mean. The authors surnames are strict alphabetical...so hers is *Cartland...C. A R T.* The authors around her will follow that. If their surname is um...*Cronin,* for instance they will come well after Cartland. CA and CR are a long way apart... follow the alphabet beyond the first letter of the last name. If we had an author called, oh let's see...um, Caaper for example, they would be filed before Cartland, because CAA comes before CAR...all the letters in the name are important when you are filing."

I wasn't sure exactly what she meant but nodded and hurried off to explore this new piece of information.

I browsed the romance section first. I began looking at the authors surnames instead of the titles. It hadn't occurred to me that they were filed in specific order.

I was trying to get a grip on what she meant. It sounded like double Dutch to me. I looked at them carefully and slowly and I could see a pattern but my brain was having trouble recognizing what it was.

I kept looking.

I still hadn't figured it out to my satisfaction when Eunice went off for her lunch break.

I made the decision to come back the next morning and for how ever many mornings it took to absorb this great new piece of information.

I was like a blank piece of blotting paper, waiting to suck in whatever landed.

Chapter 11

Jamie asked me where I'd been, which was unusual, he normally accepted that I disappeared now and then once the chores were done. I used to go into the Botanical gardens often, just to satisfy my need to be alone, with no other conversation going on around me. I liked the solitude; I needed the space. He knew about my favorite spot, yet he never intruded on me when I was there.

I didn't feel like trying to explain the new urges driving me at the moment; especially to him; it would feel like I was throwing the safety of the palace back in his face, and I couldn't bear the thought of hurting him like that.

"I was at the library."

"Un...huh. What are you reading this time?"

"Oh...All sorts of stuff."

"Like?"

"What's with the twenty questions, Jamie?"

"Nothing, Sass. Why are you so riled up? I was just making conversation, that's all."

I looked at his face and saw the worry there. He sensed something different; I know he did.

"Sorry, Jamie. I'm feeling bitchy today."

"Oh...?"

I rolled my eyes attempting to lead him in one direction without lying to him. He caught on… "Oh… oh, right. White flag time, huh?

"Mm…"

"Understood. I'll avoid you for a few days then. I value my health." He laughed and walked off, seemingly satisfied.

How the hell was I ever going to be able to tell him I wanted to leave?

I understood that he would accept it, but I doubted he would be happy about it.

And what of Baby Jenny? How could I walk away from her?

Those things ate away at me in the months that followed.

I wanted to be in a position where I could leave as soon as I'd told them I was going. Knowing full well that if I didn't do it that way…I would never be able to do it at all.

Chapter 12

It took me a week of looking at the rows upon rows of books for it to finally click in about strict alphabetical order. Once the penny dropped, I grinned happily to myself, and then hurried across to tell Eunice.

She smiled at me. "Good girl. That's the way."

"Um...Eunice...What else do Office Juniors have to do?"

Eunice looked around her to make certain nobody required her assistance before answering. "You would need to be able to follow instructions *without* answering back, young lady."

"Oops...That could be a tricky one."

She laughed, "Practice on me, dear. It might prove refreshing."

"Just like a swim bare assed in a fountain eh, Eunice?"

She gave me *the* look. I grinned and behaved myself, for the moment.

"Seriously, Sassy. Good manners are a large part of fitting into an office environment."

"What else?"

"You will be asked to make coffee, and run errands. You may be required to answer the phone, or make calls...so you need to work on your telephone technique."

"Telephone technique? I barely know how to use a bloody telephone; I haven't had the need to ring too many people, Eunice."

"You also need to work on your language skills, Sassy. Swearing is not acceptable in an office environment."

"I only said bloody!"

"That is swearing, Sassy." Eunice was looking a bit frazzled. She was giving me her time, and I was being argumentative.

"Sorry, Eunice. I appreciate your help. I have gotta learn to watch the language, and the other stuff I come out with."

"No need to police yourself too much, my dear. You have relevant thoughts to offer a lot of the time. Just mind the language. The humor is a little off, but not offensively so. I have quite gotten used to it."

I thanked her. I felt quite proud of the fact that Eunice thought my comments on some things were relevant.

I left her alone for the rest of the day. I was learning more than I dared hope and I didn't want to overdo it. After all this was her place of work, and she had already been more than generous with her time.

The next thing I needed to learn was what the hell telephone technique was.

Chapter 13

Jenny was getting taller by the day, so was I. I hit a growth spurt and was heading for the taller end of the market rapidly. I was filling out in other areas as well, which I wasn't thrilled about. Mother Nature can't be stopped by wishful thinking however.

I'm thankful that my breasts decided that small was good. For me invisible would have been better. I didn't like drawing attention to the fact that I was female.

If only it had been that simple.

Another Christmas came and went and the palace bunch had been fairly stable for quite a while. Jamie had taken on a job at night, so Flyman was in charge of the night watch now. He took it very seriously. I guess his hunger to join the army affected the way he organized things on his watch.

I resisted the urge to salute for quite a while.

When I did salute…he liked it! He liked it so much that if I forgot to do it he would look hurt and ask me why.

Flyman was one of the good guys. He was fiery tempered, but I'd never seen him lose it with one of us. His anger was normally at external things. The headlines now appearing more often in the newspapers, made him furious.

We were now seeing more and more American troops on the streets of Sydney. Apparently, we were a popular location for the Vietnam boys to spend their six days of R&R time.

Jamie said that the number of strip clubs up at the Cross had doubled, and he had never seen so many girls out working during the daylight hours. Apparently, the Yanks were a big spending bunch.

They were also big drinkers, who loved to gamble.

Organized crime was doing big business and the bag ladies were kept busy. The pay off to cops on the take was bundled together and put in a paper bag, the cops collected usually on Friday nights. The "Bourbon and Beefsteak" and "The Texas Tavern" were major collection spots, as was The Sirocco club. They were all connected by one guy, he was known as Mr. Sin. I had heard a lot about this person. One of the guys in expensive suits surrounded by his own security people, he and an acquaintance nick-named Mr. Big virtually ran the Cross back then. They were rumored to have connections to the American mafia.

I didn't want to know any more, my gut was telling me that if I asked I would find out that "Nick" from back when I lived with the woman that gave birth to me would be involved somewhere in this bunch of movers and shakers. It would be unhealthy to ask questions or even hint that I thought I knew one of these people.

I found the American boys I spoke to so courteous and curious. They were curious about everything Australian. I warned them to watch out for killer kangaroos on the main streets of Sydney and then doubled up in laughter when they took me seriously. It didn't take them long to figure that our humor down here was of the strange variety. The nightmare of Vietnam was put on hold when they came here, they partied hard, drank even harder, and the ladies of the Cross were never busier.

Tilly and Kirsty left the palace for a few months. They went back on the game and they pulled enough money to rent their own one bedroom place down in Rushcutters Bay.

They didn't last for too long back on the job however. Being without a pimp proved to be an unfriendly way to live.

They tried doing it as independents but the pimps shut them down, with threats of violence and having the other girls on the street that belonged to a stable spread the word that these particular girls would spread a dose of the clap.

Chapter 14

I had been reading the jobs available columns in the papers every Wednesday and Saturday for months and there were a large number of positions for office juniors. Problem being that most of them wanted experienced people, or a minimum education requirement of year ten.

I had already decided that if I were lucky enough to get an interview I would go across to Bondi Beach, have a hot shower, and wash my hair. I was still trying to figure out what the hell I could wear. The stuff I had was too dirty, and totally not what I saw other young people wearing as they hurried off the trains of a morning.

The clothes that had belonged to Jilly were the best I had, but they were also stained. The tiny mini-skirts would not be the best choice anyway; although most of the girls I saw in the younger aged group wore mini's they weren't bum freezers like the ones of Jilly's that I had been so generously given by Carol up at the Cross a lifetime ago.

I had visited Carol a few times over the past months, when I had finally ventured up to Kings Cross. It had been years now since the rape, and I was confident that I could handle myself if I ran into Paulie, although I always tried to go after the time he normally shut the café.

Carol wasn't always visible of course, she was a working girl and the American G.I's were everywhere.

I did manage to talk to her a couple of times, and she always seemed to know what was going on everywhere in the 'cross'.

Drew was still Carol's pimp. I couldn't help but notice how old Carol was looking. She had that look that I had come to recognize as someone on drugs of the heavy variety, heroin probably. The tell tale long sleeves in the heat of summer was an instant alert.

She was wired every time I saw her, with that nervous twitchy energy that seemed like an electrical jolt was permanently running through her veins.

I looked around at the other girls, these days they were mostly faces I didn't recognize. They all seemed to have one thing in common, they looked young; fresh meat in the supermarket from hell. Carol couldn't compete much longer. She knew it was only a matter of time before she ceased to make enough money to satisfy Drew.

I asked her what she was planning on doing after she left the business.

She looked at me as if I had asked the question in Russian or something, "Why would I leave, Sassy? I'm doin' okay."

"But what about later? You know … when you get older, I mean. What will you do then?"

"Older …? Me and some of the other girls are gonna open up a little place of our own, out in the suburbs. You can make a livin' out there, and the customers don't have to travel all the way into the city to get what they want. We know some girls that have done it, and they do okay."

"Sounds good, Carol. Why wait though? Why not do it now?"

"I've still got a few years left in me; besides there's too much money to be earned from the Yanks on R&R

leave, Sassy. They tip like you wouldn't believe. When that stops, then maybe I'll go."

She wasn't comfortable; I had pushed the question too hard and broached a subject she was avoiding thinking about. I decided to change the topic.

"I'm thinking of getting myself an office job."

"Wow … that's cool. What sort of office job?"

"Just a junior's job, you know, filing and making coffee and answering the phones … like that."

"Shit! That's a great idea, Sassy. Do ya think you can get a job like that?"

"I hope so. I'm gonna give it a shot."

"How can you get a job like that? I mean … no offence or nothin' but you aren't very clean, Sassy. Your clothes aren't either."

"Yeah, I know. I don't smell too great. I haven't figured that part all the way out yet. I think I can maybe go over to Bondi and shower at the beach. I can nick some soap and shampoo, that's easy."

"Sure. But ya clothes still stink, and they look ratty."

"I was gonna ask you if you maybe had something old that was clean. It doesn't matter if you haven't. I just don't know who else I can ask. I need a job to buy new clothes, but I need new clothes to get a job."

She nodded her head, "I should be able to come up with somethin'. So what does Jamie say about your plan?"

"Shit, Carol. Don't say anything, please. He doesn't know anything about it, not yet. I want to be able to tell him about it once I already have a job and a place to live."

"He's not gonna be happy about it, Sassy. I mean he'll be happy that you got a job and all,. But he's not gonna like you leavin'."

"It makes space for someone else." I said ... defensive as all hell.

"Jamie works nights, up here. But he's still livin' at the Palace."

"That's his choice, Carol. I'm not knocking it. He does what he does."

"Yeah, I guess. As for the clothes, I think I have something that would do. No promises mind you. I'll just see what I can do. Come back up to see me, tomorrow and we'll take a look. You'd better have a damned hot shower at my place. No point trying on anything over all that dirt."

I gave her a smelly hug. She was clearly anxious to get back to work.

I was ready to move on and said my goodbyes. I was walking away when she called me back. "Um…you know what happened that time, a few years back? With you, I mean. When you were, you know in the park." She looked uncomfortable as she spoke.

"You mean the rape?"

"Yeah … yeah. That thing."

"What about it?"

"Did ya know what happened to the guys that did that?"

"Animal told me they got beat up."

"Did he say who did it?"

"Why? Are you planning on telling, Drew?"

"Fuck, no. Besides, he already knows. We all do."

"What? Well who did it? Who beat 'em up?"

"The same person that gave you the name of Sassy. That's all I'm sayin'. You understand?"

"Fuck! Animal …? Shit, he never told me. I must be thick as a brick. I should've put two and two together. I didn't know."

"I shouldn't have said nothin'. Don't let on to him that I told ya, okay? He wanted it to be kept quiet."

"Does Jamie know?"

"I think so. Please don't say nothin', Sassy. I don't want Animal gettin' the shits with me."

"Okay. It's cool, Carol. I appreciate you telling me. Okay. I promise I'll say nothing to Animal."

"Or Jamie?"

"Or Jamie."

"Okay. I gotta get back to work. If I'm not out here, just come up and knock on the door. Unless the 'Do Not Disturb' sign is out. That means I'm taking care of business. If ya get an interview, try to make it early in the day. I normally sleep till nine. Got that?"

 "Yeah … thanks, Carol. I mean that."

She turned away, and I headed back to the palace with my head buzzing from what she'd said.

How the hell did I thank someone who had done that for me? I was in shock I guess, amazed at my own stupidity at not seeing the signs.

I wanted to acknowledge the importance of what Animal had done. How could I possibly thank him, when I wasn't supposed to know?

CHAPTER 15

I returned to the 'Cross' the next morning as planned. Carol was with a client so I left and waited just down the street and out of sight of Paulie's cafe. There were more tables outside than he used to have and nearly all of them were full of American soldiers, some with girls attached.

Business was booming apparently.

How sad that such a tragic war was adding to our economy.

I remembered the first day I had met Carol, outside Paulie's Cafe a lifetime ago.

I calculated the time as best I could remember. I had been eleven years old. It was just before I was asked to join the gang at the palace. My sixteenth birthday was now just weeks away. Five years had gone by. I could hardly believe it had been that long.

How the hell had I let so much time pass?

I gave myself a mental kick in the ass.

The newspaper said, "Junior wanted. No experience necessary. Will train. Immediate start for suitable applicant.

Apply in person."

I felt an excited jolt. The company was a well-known, reasonably large retail outlet. They were looking for someone to work in their city store. I tore the add from the paper and checked the date. The interviews were to take place in three days time.

I headed up to 'The Cross' as soon as my chores were done. Carol was still asleep and it had already gone nine o'clock. I knocked on the door as she had told me to do.

She looked dreadful without her heavy make-up, and her arms were tracked badly. She caught my look, backed into the room, and hurried me inside. I watched as she slipped on a wrap and covered her arms.

"You have an interview?"

I handed her the add. "I've got two days to get clean." I smiled at her, hoping to ease her embarrassment that I had seen her addiction.

She smiled and stood up and put the kettle on, "Coffee, Sass?"

"Oh, I'd love a coffee if you have time. I haven't had coffee in so long."

"How do you take it?"

"Milk and three sugars, thanks."

She busied herself making the coffee and I looked around her room.

It was bigger than I expected, but then I was used to the lack of any space at the palace. Carol had a large double bed, and a nice set of wardrobes with mirrors.

She was making coffee at a small sink in the corner of the room, off to the left of that was an open door, which I figured to be a shower and toilet.

"Here. You want some biscuits?"

"I never say no to food, Carol. Thanks."

We sat sipping our coffees and she lit us a couple of smokes. "So where is this interview?"

"Just down in Park Street."

"What time is it on?"

"The ad says interviews start at 9.00 o'clock."

"What address are ya gonna give 'em?"

"Shit. I don't know. I hadn't thought of that. I can't tell 'em I live in a bloody shipping container."

"Calm down." She walked over to her small bedside table and foraged around in a draw. She grunted in satisfaction and walked back to where I sat and handed me a small flyer.

"Boarding House. Cheap rates. Meals by arrangement." It gave an address down in Elizabeth Bay road. It was only a short walk, and the telephone number was on the flyer.

"Use the address. Better yet, go down and see Dulcie, see if she's got any rooms going. Lot of the girls go there when they've had enough out here. She charges fair rates, and the meals are okay. You get to share a bathroom and a kitchen. Tell her I sent you down."

"But if I don't get the job?"

"Then you don't take the room. Tell you what, I'll ring Dulcie and tell her about you. You can't go and see her the way you are now; she wouldn't let you near her place. Go and have a shower. I'll find something clean for you to wear. Dulcie normally asks for a week's rent in advance ... '

"I don't have ...."

"Go and take a shower before the stink gets into my room, we'll talk about the money later."

Carol went into the bathroom and I could hear the shower running, she came out and handed me a bar of soap still in its wrapper and a bottle of shampoo and conditioner. "Brush the knots out of your hair before you wet it, Sassy."

She handed me a brush.

"Go on ... the water won't kill you. You'll feel really nice afterwards."

I meekly did as I was told. Carol was so different; she seemed to be enjoying this. Not for pleasure though, it was as if she was helping me do what she had never been able to do herself.

The shower felt so amazing. Apart from swimming fully clothed and bathing occasionally in the fountains, I hadn't been really clean since going into the palace.

I lathered up again and again, scrubbing my skin till it stung. My hair took ages because it was so long and so very tangled. I lost a good handful of it when I finally managed to get the brush through it. It took a long time to get it clean enough so the shampoo would lather.

I dried off, and wrapped a towel around my wet hair. I felt so damned good. Carol handed me a wrap to put on, and she put the kettle on again.

When she'd made the coffee she gave me mine and passed a smoke across. "Well, now. You had a pretty face hiding under all that dirt. You have grown up, haven't you, Sass? So you'd be what, twenty-twenty one by now?"

"I'm almost sixteen."

"Fuck! What? Fuck me dead, you can't be! You've been out here for what ... four years?"

"I was eleven when I met you at Paulies, Carol."

"Oh, Jesus. I'm so sorry, Sassy. I knew you were young, but I figured fifteen or sixteen, you know. You seemed so ... so, together."

"I play poker real good as well."

She grinned.

"Well let's get you dressed. I have to get ready to go to work myself."

"This is some stuff I keep separate for when I go and visit my family. I've worn all of it a few times, so I need to buy some more um ... conservative things anyway."

She handed me a pair of jeans and a pretty blue top. The jeans were a little tight, but not uncomfortably so. The top fit just fine.

I had no shoes that would pass inspection. And she didn't have anything that would fit except a pair of flip-flops. They were better than nothing, and almost fit.

I towel dried my long hair, and Carol plaited it in one long plait that hung down my back. "That'll keep it from tangling up so much." She said.

"Right, let's look at you." She walked me over to the closet and opened it to the full-length mirror on the inside.

I barely recognized myself. Mirrors and I hadn't been familiar companions out here.

I looked at the tall dark haired girl with the big eyes in the mirror and blinked.

I didn't look like a kid anymore. I looked like a woman. That scared me more than a little.

"You like?" asked Carol.

"I ... I don't know. I didn't know I looked like that. But, thanks again, Carol. I don't know how I can ever repay all your kindness."

"You wanna know how?"

"Yes! Yes I do ... please tell me."

"Get off these fuckin' streets, Sassy. Get as far away as you can and don't ever, ever come back. I want you to do that. For me ... and for Jilly. I think you can do it, Sassy. You have something inside you that I don't have. I don't know what you call it, and it doesn't matter, but you know it. You've known it since the day I met you at Paulies.

"Get yourself a fuckin' job, and a life. That's what I want." She had tears streaming down her face and made no attempt to hide them.

"Carol ... why don't you ..."

"Don't, Sassy. It's too late for me. I don't have the strength to do it, and I never did. That's it. No more talk. Dulcie is expecting you. I don't know your real name and I don't want too. She is expecting a friend of mine named Sassy. That's all. Now off you go. I'll see you early on Tuesday morning; you can shower and get dressed for the interview here. I'll do your hair."

She put her hand in the middle of my back and steered me towards the door.

"See you, Tuesday."

"Yeah, Tuesday. I ..."

She had already closed the door.

I'd forgotten all about how good it felt to be clean, and smell good.

The dehumanizing process takes only a short while out on the streets.

Even in the relative safety of the palace, you tend to behave like those around you. You blend in. They are dirty so you are dirty.

No one wants to stand out. Doing that sort of thing makes enemies.

I had found over time that my penchant for standing up for certain members in the group had created problems for me with some of the others anyway.

Looking different would have set me apart too much.

I found the boarding house with no trouble and rang the front bell.

The biggest dog I had ever seen bounded out of it when it opened, nearly knocking me off my feet.

He was huge. I knelt down and called him over, and had another face wash free of charge. He wiggled and snuffled and drooled all over me ... I laughed.

"Well then ... you passed that test. Major! Down!" The voice boomed. I had never heard a woman with such a deep voice before.

I stood up and looked up and up. The biggest, ugliest, loudest women I had ever met stood there.

"I'm Dulcie," she announced. "You must be Sassy. G'day." She stuck out a hand that Big Mike would be proud of.

My own hand was swallowed in a hard grip. "C'mon I'll show you the rooms. I got two available at the moment. You can choose which you want. Price is the same."

I followed the mountainous women down a long hallway that had a number of doors off each side.

She opened one door and I was surprised how big the room was. It had one large window that looked out at the brick wall next door. It was sparsely furnished with a single bed, a bedside table with a lamp, and a dressing table and small closet. It was spotlessly clean.

The second room was much smaller and further away from the shared inside toilet and bathroom, but it had a small porch that came off the bedroom and looked over the garden at the back. The porch was only accessible from the bedroom. I loved it. The room was smaller but the porch and the privacy it gave the occupant won me.

"Oh, I love this one." I said

"Yeah ... thought you might. You can smoke out on the porch, but not in the room. No guests overnight. You can use the kitchen for your meals. There's a jug in your room and a small sink. So you can make coffee and stuff. You need to label anything you put in the fridge. The top shelf is for your stuff, you'll share the shelf with Norman. He's in the room next door to you closest to the kitchen. I supply meals but at a cost, we can talk about that some more if you take the room."

"Did Carol tell you I'm applying for a job on Tuesday? I have no idea how I'll go with that. I can't pay a week in advance. I don't know yet what the pay is and if I can afford the room." I finished in a rush.

"Carol offered to pay the week in advance, if you get the job. You can sort that out with her. I'll keep the room until Friday night. But if someone wants it after that I'll let 'em take it. Understood?"

"Understood."

"Good. Phone me or come around and tell me what's happening by Friday night. Good luck with the job."

Dulcie escorted me back to the front door where I was lovingly farewelled and slurped over again by the dog.

I thought about Carol and her generosity. I was so saddened by the fact that nobody had done the same thing for her when she ended up here.

Now I had to go back to the palace and explain why I was so clean and well dressed.

I was dreading it.

Chapter 16

I arrived back at the palace and went in search of Jamie.

Jenny came over to me with a question and a smile on her face. "Sassy? Wow, you look so cool. What happened? You're clean too, and you smell good."

"It's a long story, baby girl. I'll tell you all about it later. Have you seen Jamie?"

"He'll be back soon he said. He's doin' somethin' for Big Mike. How come you're all dressed up?" This time the question had a quiver to it as if it had suddenly dawned on Jenny that this somehow indicated a change was in the air.

Change terrified Jenny. Any change. She needed everything around her to be absolutely predictable. Even predictably bad was better than something altering.

"You're really pretty!" it was an accusation.

"We'll keep that our secret. Okay?"

She gave me her lovely smile. I looked at her face noticing for the first time that her cheeks had filled out, and the first bloom of young womanhood was there to see under the dirt.

A few of the others had come in and I got some good-natured ribbing from the lot of them. I was edgy; I needed to speak to Jamie before someone asked me a question I didn't want to answer.

I walked back outside and strolled down to the water's edge. I sat there alone for a while absorbing everything around me and committing it to memory. I was taking a mental snapshot of what I hoped to soon be leaving behind.

Doubts invaded my thought process. I had no idea what was waiting for me outside the relative safety of the palace. I simply knew that I had to give myself a chance to find out if I could make it away from here.

My heart was heavy. This place wouldn't be hard to leave, but the people were another thing entirely. I had no idea if I could force myself to stay away, or if I wouldn't come scampering back if I couldn't deal with being in the world outside again.

I turned as I became aware I was being watched. Jamie was standing a couple of yards away smoking. I gave him a hesitant smile.

"Well, I thought that was you." He said walking towards me. He sat on the edge of the dock next to me and handed me a lit cigarette.

I inhaled deeply, composing myself as best I could.

"So when are you going, Sass?"

"You know?"

"It's been coming a while, I've watched you, and I've seen that look on your face. What's the plan?"

"I want to get an office job. There's interviews on Tuesday. I have no idea how I'll do. But I have to give it a try, Jamie. It's ... it's getting too easy to forget about the stuff I want to do with my life. If I stay much longer, I'll never be able to go. Do you understand that?"

"Yeah, yeah, Sass. I get it. I knew it would be only a matter of time with you. Those dreams of yours are strong. You're strong. I believe you can make a go of anything you set your stubborn mind to. Well maybe not brain surgery." He was trying to laugh but it seemed to get caught in his throat.

"Can I ask you something really personal?" I said softly.

"You can ask. No guarantee you'll get an answer though."

"You have a paying night job. Why are you still here?"

"I thought about leaving. I thought about it a lot. I don't know if this'll make a whole lot of sense, but I'm happy here. I'm putting away most of my earnings, breaking my own rules about sharing everything into the bargain. When I leave, I want to have enough contacts and be earning enough to buy a place of my own. I reckon on another year or so and I should be in a situation when I can make a good down payment. Living here and putting away every cent I earn will almost guarantee it."

"What sort of place? A home?"

"Yeah. A home I can run a business from."

"What sort of business?"

"Security. That's what I do at night."

"What sort of security? You mean being a bouncer?"

"That's just the surface stuff, Sassy. That's all I'm saying about it. Okay?"

"Yes, sure. Thanks ... I thought you'd tell me to mind my own damned business."

"That has never stopped you before now, has it?"

"Nope."

"I'll miss you, Sassy."

"I can't say anything until I have a job to go to, Jamie. Especially to Jenny; Jamie, what will happen to her when you leave?"

"If she's still here I'll take her with me, Sassy. She'll never make it without someone watching over her. But I can't force her to come. I hope you get a job soon. Jenny is not going to handle this at all well."

Tuesday came faster than I wanted it to. My nerves had my stomach twisted in a tight knot. I got up extra early and fetched the water for everyone. Trying to act as if this day was no more important than any other.

Jamie gave me a nod and a whispered good luck

I headed up to see Carol.

She was awake and waiting for me when I arrived. She put the kettle on while I had a shower and washed my hair. Then she blow-dried it and styled it really nicely.

She had laid out a few things that she thought might be suitable for an interview. A couple of the skirts were way to short. I had long legs and they were too exposed to my way of thinking. There was a pair of black bell bottomed trousers, which fit really well. They looked smart and fresh. The blouse was a peach colour and hung in soft folds over the hips. I figured the trousers would hide the fact that I was wearing flip flops pretty well.

I barely recognized the female in the mirror, and only hoped that the look of terror on my face would disappear when I got down to the place the interviews were being held.

Carol practically shoved me out the door after a quick hug.

There were three other girls waiting when I arrived. I checked out what they were wearing and felt good about what Carol and I had picked out. I felt I would pass muster okay, at least visually.

The time seemed to stop, and I felt sick to my stomach.

Then the other girls were gone and I was next.

A well-dressed woman came out and smiled at me, standing back to allow me to walk past her and into an office. I sat where she indicated.

"Good morning, I'm Miss Atkins. What is your name, please?" she had a pen poised over a clipboard.

"Good morning. My name is Stacey ... Stacey Danson." My voice sounded like it was buried somewhere and trying to dig its way out.

"Is this your first interview, Stacey?"

"Yes."

"Don't be nervous. I don't bite, dear."

I smiled ... I think.

Miss Atkins handed me the clipboard and a pen. "Please complete this form, Stacey. I'll leave you to do that, and be back shortly."

"Thank you." I squeaked.

The beginning of the form was easy enough. My name and address. The next line and the remainder of the form stopped me dead in my tracks.

Last school attended?

Level attained?

Three personal references:

"Shit!" I was ready to get the fuck out of there fast. I wasn't prepared. Not for this type of information.

Miss Atkins came back in and I was sitting there feeling like a damned idiot.

She put her hand out for the clipboard.

I stood up. "I'm sorry I wasted your time." I managed to say.

"Sit down, dear. Let me take a look. Then I'll decide if you wasted my time or not."

I sat.

"What is it about the form that is unclear, dear?" she asked kindly.

"Oh, it's not unclear, not at all. It's just ... um ... I don't have that information." I finished lamely; wishing a hole in the floor would open up and let me disappear.

"You don't know what high school you attended?" She asked in amazement; already relegating me to the mentally impaired slot.

I thought about lying. I scrambled to think of something that would sound right. I couldn't come up with a single damned thing that would sound believable.

"I didn't go to high school." I stood again.

"Sit down, dear. What do you mean; you didn't go to high school?"

"Look. I appreciate that you are busy. But I'm not what you are after. Okay? I don't have three references either. So, you know. It's better that I go."

"Well ... of course if you feel that way my dear. Can I ask you why you applied for the job before you leave?"

"Why? I want to work. I want to learn stuff. I need a job. That's about it."

"Where is this address you have given?" she asked

"It's a proper address. A boarding house."

"How long have you lived there?"

"If I get the job, I'll be living there from Friday."

"Where are you currently living?"

"With friends."

"Not with your family?"

That did it. This time I stood up and stuck out my hand. She took it and gave me a confused smile.

"Thanks for seeing me." I walked out of the office, out of the building and headed rapidly for the botanical gardens.

I went to the sandstone overhang that had always given me peace and shelter.

I cried until I couldn't cry anymore.

I couldn't face anybody right then. My thoughts were all over the place. I felt gutted. I had so much pinned on the outcome of that interview. At the time, I didn't think about how to go about getting the sort of information required on the application, because it didn't exist.

I couldn't fill that in on a form.

As for the three personal references. The people I knew well enough to vouch for me weren't exactly citizens that would invoke a lot of enthusiasm in a prospective employer.

I had no idea what I was going to do. I did know however that I needed to be alone to try and work out what to do next.

For the first time in almost five years, I didn't go back to the palace.

I slept in the gardens just as I had done all those years before.

I was woken by a furiously angry Jamie as dawn was breaking.

I had never seen him so worked up.

"What the fuck are you tryin' to do, Sassy? We are all worried sick that somethin' happened to you!" He screamed at me.

"Whoa! Shit! Back off, Jamie." I stood up and stepped back away from him.

"Jenny is cryin' her bloody eyes out! Nobody can sleep. You know fuckin' better than that!"

I had never seen him this angry.

"I take it the bloody interview was a bust?" He was still screaming.

I remained silent.

"Well? What the fuck happened?"

"I'll tell you when you have calmed down."

"Calmed down! Right, of course, it's not like I actually give a fuck about what might have happened to you or anthing!"

"Jamie ... I'm sorry you were worried. That's all. I won't talk to you in this mood."

He looked ready to explode again. He stomped off a few yards and stopped. I saw the flare of the cigarette lighter and waited. He lit up twice more and smoked them before he came back over to where I was sitting.

"Well? What happened?" he had his temper held in check.

"Too many bloody questions I couldn't answer, that's about it. I couldn't tell 'em what High school I went to, 'cause I never went. I don't have an address that I already live at that I can give; and they wanted 3 personal references!"

"Fuck!"

"You got that right."

"So, you have to get 'em that information. I don't know what to do about the High School thing. But can't you give 'em a fake address?"

"They wanted a phone number so they could check."

"Fuck!"

"I got somewhere lined up, in case I got the job. But that'll be gone after Friday."

"Where at?"

"Carol gave me the number of a boarding house down in Elizabeth Bay."

"Dulcie's place?"

"Yeah, how did you know?"

"Dulcie is kinda well known."

"I am beginning to get that idea myself. Besides that, who can I get as references? I reckon all the jobs I can try for will ask the same sort of stuff."

"What about the woman at the Library?"

"Eunice? Shit, she might do it for me. But she doesn't know me all that well, really."

"Tell me something then. Who apart from me and Jenny would you have spoken to the most over the past four bloody years?"

"Carol ... and Animal, and ... . Yeah, yeah you're right, Eunice."

"So?"

"So, thanks. I'll go up when the Library opens."

"Wash your face first. The rest of you looks good, but your eyes look like a Panda bear, with all that black goop everywhere."

"Mascara."

"Yeah, that black goop."

"So, am I forgiven for making you worry like that?"

"I forgive you, only 'cause you would have been pretty upset. You just weren't thinkin'. But Jenny might take some convincing. She's gonna take you leavin' really hard; you know that don't you?"

"I know. But I can't let that stop me, I'm afraid I'll never do it if I don't do it soon, Jamie."

He looked unbearably sad for a moment. "Yeah, I know."

I went with him back to the palace, and was greeted by silence. Jenny was asleep wrapped around her doll, and the kids that were awake picked up on Jamie's mood and kept quiet.

His temper had deflated somewhat but his edginess was obvious.

It was almost full sunrise, and I couldn't sleep anyway so I headed back outside and sat on the dock again.

The changes were already happening and the consequences were going to cause some strain in the group.

Jenny found me outside when she woke up. She sat next to me on the dock. "Where were you, Sass?"

"I had some stuff I had to think through quietly, Jen. I needed some space to do it in. That's all."

"Jamie was angry."

"Yeah, I know. I should've let you guys know what I was going to do, so you wouldn't be worried."

"Is everything okay now?"

"It's fine, honey."

She looked at me to confirm that, and looked away quickly. She could sense that something was different and I had nothing I could say to her then that wouldn't be a lie if she asked me any more questions.

I couldn't tell her I was leaving until I was about to go. It didn't matter how I said it, for Jenny it would be a major change in her life and change was something she feared.

******

I left the palace and stopped by Carol's place to fill her in on what had happened, but the Do Not Disturb sign on her door didn't allow for that. I decided to try again after I'd been to see Eunice.

I headed up to the library in time for it to open.

Eunice looked surprised when I walked in. I had forgotten that she had never seen me clean and wearing clothes that didn't stink.

"My word, Sassy, you look so different I barely recognized you."

"I'm clean."

"Yes, that's quite obvious, my dear."

"I had an interview yesterday, Eunice and it didn't go so well."

"Give me a moment, and we'll chat, dear. I have a few things I must do before we get busy."

"Thanks, Eunice."

I headed over to the shelves and looked at nothing in particular. My thoughts were churning around in my head, and I wasn't at all sure I felt right about asking Eunice for a reference. I guess I was worried she'd say no, or laugh. Which on reflection was pretty damned unfair of me, she had always treated me kindly, I had no reason to suppose she would be any different.

She beckoned me over after 15 minutes or so. "So tell me all about it. What went wrong, specifically?"

"The lady doing the interview was nice enough. But the form I had to fill in threw me into a spin."

"How so?"

"They asked me what high school I attended and what level I had reached just for starters, and my permanent address and how long I'd lived there. Then they wanted three personal references. I walked out."

"Were you rude?"

"No ... no ... at least I don't think so. I said I was sorry I had wasted their time; then I left."

"I am sorry, Sassy. That would have been embarrassing for you."

"It was. I was wondering if you would feel okay about writing me a personal reference, Eunice." I got out in a rush, and waited for the no.

"I don't have a real problem with that my dear. I have known you for quite some time, haven't I?"

"Yes, it's been a while. I know you don't really know me, but anything would be a help I think."

"Yes. Can you leave it with me, dear? I will need to think through what I write. I will do it at home on my own time. Pop back in tomorrow and I will try and have it done and typed up for you. What address did you use, Sassy?"

"A boarding house down in Elizabeth Bay. I've organized a room, but I have to let it go if I don't have a job by Friday."

"I see. That would be a shame, but there would be other places like it surely?"

"I don't know. I haven't looked yet."

"Well I suggest you check out a few more, dear. Do you have any other interviews lined up?"

"No. Not yet. I figured they are all gonna ask the same damned questions, I haven't got answers for."

"Hmm. Very well, I must get back to work. I shall see you tomorrow."

"Thanks, Eunice. Thanks a lot."

She called me back, "Sassy, I don't know your real name dear. I can hardly write a reference without it."

Eunice waited for an answer, I had no real choice. Inventing another name was just going to complicate things even more. "It's Stacey Danson, Eunice."

"Is that the name you are putting on your resume, dear?"

"Yeah, it's my name."

She nodded and said no more.

I headed off, acutely aware of the fact that the people I felt closest to, like Jamie and Jenny, Carol and Animal … none of them knew my real name.

The thought made me sad. We were all hiding behind our street names. I would need to learn to stop doing that when I left the streets. Although I figured that as some folks had nick names, Sassy was as good as any.

I left feeling a little more positive about myself. I headed for Hyde Park and grabbed Wednesday's copy of the Herald. It was full of jobs, but not one of them required no experience.

Chapter 17

The next morning I caught up with Carol and filled her in on what was happening.

Then I dropped in at the boarding house to let Dulcie know that the room was a no go unless by some miracle I landed a job that day or the next. Dulcie understood, and merely commented that she hadn't exactly been rushed for the spare rooms, so I might still get lucky later in the week.

I arrived at the library later than usual and Eunice was extremely busy.

She gave me a smile and a wave indicating that I should come over to the desk.

"Good morning, Stacey. I wonder, dear, if you could do something for me, this stack of books needs to be placed back on the shelves. Would you help me out by doing that for me? You know now how they are kept."

The stack was large. I was more than happy to help her in any way I could, so I nodded yes.

"Anything you're not certain about just bring it back to the desk for me. Thank you, dear."

"Sure, Eunice. That's cool."

I grabbed six off the stack and took them over to a desk. I figured to place them in order of fiction and non-fiction to start with, and then by type. Genre was still a word I was not familiar with back then.

I took my time about doing it, not wishing to do the wrong thing and let her down. I was happy that she trusted me enough to do this, although puzzled as to why one of her assistants wasn't delegated to the task.

The stack on her desk was almost completed before she was free of people at the desk.

"Almost done, Stacey?"

"Yep. Almost. Just these couple more to do."

"Fine, thank you, dear. That has saved me some time. When you have finished come back over so we can have a chat. All right?"

"Sure."

I had another hour or so of double-checking myself to make certain I had done the right thing, then walked over to her and waited for her to look up from what she was doing.

"All done?"

I nodded.

"Marvellous."

She looked around, no one was hovering waiting for her attention, and she grinned at me. "Okay. Now young woman we need to discuss telephone technique."

"Yeah, what is that? It sounds hard."

"No it is not difficult at all, dear. It's all about good manners. When you answer a telephone what do you say?"

"Um ... I don't remember if I have ever answered one, Eunice. I guess I'd probably say ... um, hello?"

She looked a little shocked.

"Oh, my word. I am sorry, dear; I should have realized that you wouldn't exactly have access to a telephone. It's not difficult at all. Just remember that the person calling the number should be greeted politely and then have confirmed for them that they have the right number."

"So, I say what? Hello ... um ... this is the library."

"Not exactly. Firstly, you greet them with a Good Morning or Good Afternoon, and then you can say either "State Library ... or your name, as in 'Stacey speaking' Then you say, 'May I help you?'"

"That makes sense, sort of. But I wouldn't know how to help them. So what do I do then?"

"Good girl. When they have told you what they want, you ask them to please hold the line, and you give the call to whomever it is that can assist them. In this case me. Once you have done that and passed the message along, you thank them for waiting and tell them that someone will be with them in a moment. Good manners are all it takes, Stacey. You treat the person on the telephone with courtesy at all times."

"What if they don't treat me with courtesy? I hang up, right?"

"No, dear. It would be unusual to have someone less than courteous ring here, dear. However if that does happen, don't hang up. Just say 'one moment please' and pass me the phone. Okay?"

"Yeah, I guess."

I glared at the black telephone just in case.

"So. You can take the next call."

"Oh ... maybe I hadn't better do that, 'till I practise."

"The best way to learn is to do it, my dear. I'll be right here. Better yet, I will telephone this number from the reading area, and you can practise on me. How about that idea?"

"Phew, yeah, that'd be cool, but you know, give me a minute."

"One thing you must learn to do, Stacey is never let a phone ring for too long. Try to answer it before the third ring, if you are busy with someone else you excuse yourself, and then say 'one moment please'. The call should never go unanswered. You will find that there will always be someone helping wherever you work during the busy times of the day.

"Right. We'll do this during my lunch break. Come back at 1.00 o'clock dear."

"Great! I will. This is so cool, thanks heaps Eunice."

I was excited. I loved learning new things. I headed off to the park to pick up the daily paper. I had begun reading the paper cover to cover, except for sport. I just didn't get the idea of grown people playing games; at least not ball games. I figured you'd have to trust the people you were playing with to do the right thing and make the right moves. Team sports were definitely on my "I don't understand this shit list."

The time dragged as it always did when I was anxious about something.

I was back at the library exactly on time. Eunice smiled at me as I bounced over to the desk. I must have looked like a puppy ready for walkies time.

She had set up an area ready for me to do my practise telephone techniques, well away from the common area of the library.

I had a writing pad handed to me with the instructions clearly noted. Eunice would have made a wonderful teacher.

The phone rang and I jumped. I grabbed it and babbled something.

"Slow it down, dear. No point in answering a call if the person on the other end doesn't understand a word you've said. Let's do it again."

This time I made a conscious effort to slow down my response, but forgot to ask 'may I help you'.

Eunice appeared to be enjoying herself hugely. We practised for her entire lunch break, and I was feeling quite confident by the end of the hour.

She gave the phone one more ring. And I responded with "Good morning, City Morgue, Bea Stiff speaking."

Eunice's laugh rang out, and she turned red and kept right on giggling in a very un-Eunice type fashion.

I figured I had this telephone technique stuff nailed.

Eunice returned to her desk and her manner again became very professional, although she was still a little red in the face.

"I must focus on my work now, Stacey. I want you to come back again during my lunch break tomorrow, dear.

I can show you a few other small things that should assist you in any form of office work. Can you be here?"

"Absolutely! Thanks again, Eunice. You are just so ... cool."

"I don't recall ever being told I am cool before, Stacey. Thank you. I assume that is a compliment?"

"The biggest!"

She smiled and began to busy herself at the desk, which was my cue to leave.

"Stacey? I'll have that reference for you on Friday."

I had forgotten all about the reference. "Great! See you tomorrow."

She nodded. I left and headed back to the palace, eager to tell Jamie about the events of my day.

Chapter 18

Jamie wasn't at the palace when I got back. I was careful not to seem too excited about the day I had just had. I was concerned mostly about Jenny's reaction to what would eventually mean me leaving.

I knew that Jamie intended to ask her to go with him when he ultimately left, but that wouldn't avert the scene I knew was coming. I had racked my brain trying to work out a way I could have her with me when I went, wherever it was I was going.

I hadn't been able to get past the thought that she would need to be alone when I was working. Plus I doubted that any boarding house would allow two for one rates.

Jenny needed a familiar environment. She had a shot at that if she was with Jamie. My future was uncertain at best. I couldn't ask her to come with me, knowing that in advance.

Jamie was late getting back, he'd had some work that needed doing after hours, and that was all he would say on the matter.

I joined him outside near the fire; we were both reluctant to say too much. The tense silence between us was both unfamiliar and unwelcome.

I wanted to share my excitement with him about the things I had learned that day, but he was clearly not in a talkative mood.

He broke the silence finally. "Any luck on the job front?"

"No, nothing in the paper that didn't ask for previous experience."

"It'll happen. Just be patient, Sass. There is no rush for you to leave is there?"

"No ... not really. I guess. I'm ... well, I'm worried. If I don't make a move soon, Jamie, I may never do it."

"You'll do it, Sassy. This was never more than a safe place to be for you until you were ready to go it alone. It just seemed to happen so quickly, I wasn't prepared for it. Then when I looked at it it hit me that you and Jenny have been here the longest now, except for me."

"Those years disappeared."

"Yeah, they did. If you aren't ready to go now, you probably never will be, Sassy. I'm being selfish wanting you to stay. I know that. I don't wanna lose you. Lose touch with you I mean." He corrected himself and looked away.

"We'll have to try and make sure that doesn't happen, Jamie. I will always want to know how you and Jenny are doing, and the others .You guys are the only family I really have."

"I think it's a good idea for us to stay in touch, Sassy. But I'd be lying to you if I were to say that's always gonna be the way it is. When you begin something new for yourself sometimes it's better to just cut the old life off."

"That would be like cutting my arm off, Jamie. You and the others are a big part of me. How can you even think I would be able to just walk away?"

He didn't answer. He just nodded and lit up a smoke.

Jamie was far wiser than I was about what could and couldn't remain in my life. He knew that at best the contact would be brief and unconnected to whatever else I did. It was wishful thinking on my part to believe things wouldn't change.

Eunice was pleased to see me when I finally arrived.

Jenny had been crying all night again, and our efforts to calm her ended in more tears. She was avoiding talking to me now, and it hurt like hell, but I understood why. Poor baby was scared to death, and nothing I could say reassured her that everything would be fine. She wanted me to say I would never leave. That was something I simply couldn't do.

Eunice had my reference ready and it was simply wonderful. I wish I had kept a copy of it. She had been so clever the way she worded it, saying that circumstances had denied me a high school education but that through hard work and a desire to learn I had managed to secure for myself good reading and writing skills and a thirst for knowledge.

She also said that I had worked in the Library on a volunteer basis from time to time and had a pleasant telephone manner, which would prove beneficial to any prospective employer.

I giggled when I read that bit. "So that's what the filing and the phone thing was about?"

She smiled at me and went a little red in the face, "Well, you did exactly what I said. Did you not?"

I laughed again, "Eunice you are the coolest of the cool."

"Why thank you, dear." She said turning even redder.

She had run off ten copies of the reference, and placed them in a plastic sleeve.

Typed on the library letterhead they looked impressive to me.

The age of the computer was still a good way off. Typewriters and carbon copies were still the way of things, although the library boasted a photocopying machine.

Eunice got back to her work after extracting a promise that I would let her know as soon as I had another interview lined up.

******

Another week went by without anything appearing in the paper that I was game to apply for.

I was getting downhearted about the office job idea, and had decided to apply for any job at all, including shop and waitressing work. They would give me experience and that could only be a good thing. I don't think I was being sensible restricting myself to applying only for office jobs; I just had an image of myself as a well-dressed office worker, like it was a ticket to acceptability, or something. I realized that was fucking stupid, finally. A job was a job, and I could still go for interviews for other positions in lunch breaks. I began looking at all available jobs for junior staff.

The time was passing and Jenny calmed down, I was still with them in the palace and for her all was right with the world.

I had been so caught up with my own thoughts that I hadn't noticed that Kirsty wasn't looking at all well. It was only when Jamie asked me if she had lost weight that I took a good look. She had ... and not just a small amount of weight either.

Tilly was hovering around her all the time and Kirsty wasn't her usual blustering larger than life self.

Jamie called Tilly aside and asked her what was going on, she cried when she started to talk about how worried she was. Kirsty was eating the same amount of food but still losing weight. Plus she was tired all the time, needing to sleep more and more during the day.

Jamie tried talking to Kirsty with no luck; he asked me to see if I could get more information out of her. Kirsty and I got on really well together, and had similar dispositions as in 'no bullshit please'.

I waited till she was on her own and cornered her, shocked at what my busy eyes had failed to see. She looked ill, very ill.

I sat next to her. "So, you're sick girl. What's happening?"

"Nothin' ... I'm okay, Sassy."

"Yeah? Bullshit! Come on Kirsty, what's goin' on?"

She looked at me long and hard. "I don't know. Okay? I just feel like shit all the time."

"Are you in pain? Anywhere?"

"No! ... Well yeah, a little maybe, but I don't think it's anything to worry about. The tiredness is the worst thing. I just wanna sleep all the time and I keep throwing up every time I eat."

"Are you pregnant?"

"Shit no! Do I look stupid to you?"

"No, not stupid, just bloody sick. You need to see a doctor, Kirsty."

"No I don't."

"Yes, Kirsty love, you do."

"Like you do when you get that horrible pain thing?"

"That's different."

"Why?"

"Because I'm hiding. You and Tilly aren't."

"Well ... yeah, but I still don't wanna see no doctor."

"You're scared aren't you? That's understandable, Kirsty love. But it might be somethin' real simple and you have probably been all worried and worrying Tilly for nothing, eh?"

"You think it might be somethin' easy fixed?" She looked hopeful.

"I don't know, love. But if it is you would be silly to put yourself and everyone else through the worry, wouldn't you?"

"I guess. Maybe I'll go up to the emergency room at the hospital, doesn't cost nothing that way." She was grudging about it, but I knew once she said she'd do something she always followed through.

I felt terrible that I hadn't noticed her not being well, I was so caught up in my own needs.

"So, I'll tell Tilly, okay? You know how much she loves you. It will make her feel better as well to know nothing bad is going on. Won't it?"

"She worries too much."

"No such thing when you love someone, mate."

Kirsty smiled.

I went outside and told Jamie and Tilly she would go up to the hospital.

Jamie now had access to a car if he needed one. We didn't ask how, and he didn't volunteer the information. He went to get it, and we helped Kirsty up and she washed her face and hands.

The weight loss was even more noticeable when she stood up. The jeans that were usually tight on her were baggy around the bum and thighs.

Jamie got back in around half an hour with the car and he took both the girls up to the hospital emergency room.

Kirsty never came back home to the palace. The cancer was in her Lymph glands and had already progressed too far. She underwent chemotherapy and radiation therapy, and then called a stop to it. The hospice wasn't far; Tilly was there every day for as many hours as Kirsty could handle visitors. The rest of us went in shifts over the weeks that followed. Kirsty was sleeping most of the time, the drugs mercifully keeping her almost pain free.

Tilly was with her when she died.

Kirsty's parents asked that Tilly and the rest of *"you people"* respect their wishes and not attend the funeral. They intended to keep to the lie they had created when they threw Kirsty out of their house for being a 'dyke'. To everyone's knowledge, Kirsty had been travelling overseas and broadening her education when she fell ill.

Jamie spent a lot of his hard earned dollars and we all got totally drunk the night she died. We toasted our missing friend and exchanged highly graphic accounts of some of the trouble Kirsty and her zest for life had gotten her and everyone else into.

The anger we felt surfaced and we reluctantly accepted the fact that we were always going to be '*you people*' to outsiders that wouldn't or couldn't defend the family they were meant to love unconditionally.

Tilly may as well have died with her darling Kirsty that day; she was a barely functioning shadow of herself without that brilliant light that Kirsty had lit within her.

She ate, drank and slept on autopilot, and nothing we could do helped to lighten her sorrow. Tilly left the palace and went back on the game. We caught up with her every so often when she dropped in to see us.

Four months after Kirsty passed away, Tilly overdosed on heroin.

She left a note for her parents.

The mood in the palace was dark and sombre. Nobody seemed to laugh anymore.

Jenny started lashing out at everyone and anyone. Her pain surfacing with force and directed at the only people who had ever shown her love. We understood the anger; it was something we all shared. We loved her, so we didn't lash back. She needed to rid herself of all that poisonous hate she carried with her all the time, and she was secure enough in her knowledge that we cared to pour that poison on us.

It broke my heart to hear her.

******

I had been to three interviews in the 2 months after Kirsty died. None of them successful. The shop work would have been okay, but they felt I was not the type they were looking for. Whatever that was.

I popped into the Library once a week, and Eunice had taken to bringing extra sandwiches at lunchtime on a Thursday. She and I sat outside on a bench under the trees and we talked. I loved those lunch sessions; Eunice was older than I thought she was at forty-three. We talked about her trips overseas and she shared photographs of some of the places she'd been.

Eunice had never married, although she admitted she had been asked a few times. She was an independent woman in an age where that was only just becoming an acceptable way to be.

I got the feeling that she was lonely, but content to be that way. She had friends that were married that kept trying to pair her off with someone or other. That made her 'very cross' as she put it.

She had never had a child, but she had nieces and nephews who she spoiled. She also owned her home, and was owned herself by a horde of stray cats and dogs that she lavished her affection on.

I had circled an ad in the paper that I was interested in applying for and showed it to her.

"This one looks promising, Stacey."

"I thought it looked okay, can't shoot me for trying, eh, Eunice?"

The job was as an office junior, no experience necessary, training provided. It was in the office of a large retail store that offered hire purchase accounts to valued clients, or so the add said.

Eunice let me use the phone on her desk to make the appointment.

I was nervous as always, but at least I was clean and reasonably presentable. I had taken to only filling out my name and address on the form {Eunice let me use her address as my place of residence on the forms now.} I would hand them my reference from Eunice with the form and wait.

Usually the person would read the reference and say it was excellent, and in the next breath tell me why I wasn't suitable for the position. What a weird world it was, I was told when applying for the shop jobs that I would probably be bored very quickly as the work could be tedious, and perhaps not what I was after.

This one went a little differently. The woman read the reference and nodded. She asked me when I would be available to commence if I were to be offered the position, and I told her I could make an immediate start.

She shook my hand, which was different, and asked me to telephone late that next afternoon, as she still had quite a few people to interview. She assured me she would let me know then if I had been successful.

I was on edge and hopeful, the interview felt different this time.

I headed back to the palace and Jamie was up and around. He slept during the days now, and worked at night. The guard on the palace at night was switched once a week. I had been taking my turn for quite a while. I liked sitting outside by the fire at night, and always had one of the others, usually one of the guys for company.

Jamie looked at me and grinned, "Well?"

"I don't know yet, I'll find out late tomorrow."

"What do you think?"

"I don't wanna get my hopes up, Jamie. But this one felt different.

*****

I headed up to the library late in the afternoon the next day. Eunice wished me good luck as I dialled the number.

Mrs. O'Keeffe was the name of the woman that had conducted the interview, I was informed that she was on another call, and would be with me shortly.

She came to the phone and I asked her if I had been successful and held my breath. She said. "When can you start, Stacey?"

"Pardon?"

"The position is yours, Stacey. Congratulations. Will you be free to begin on Monday morning?"

"Yes, thank you. Monday of course, of course ..um ... yes. What time should I come? Do I see you again?" I started to babble.

"Yes, Stacey. Be here at 8.00 am dear. I will introduce you around and we'll get you started."

"Thank you so much." I think I managed to squeal.

I turned to Eunice and she was smiling broadly. I forgot where the hell I was and grabbed her in an altogether unexpected hug. "I got it ... I got the job, I got it!" Eunice hugged me back.

"Congratulations, Stacey. I am so pleased for you, dear." She had tears in her eyes, which prompted another big hug from me.

"Eunice, Thank you! If it hadn't been for your help and ... and that reference I would never have got it."

"When do you start?" she asked still smiling hugely.

"Monday morning at 8.00 am sharp."

"Well that is wonderful news. That also gives you a few days to organize somewhere to live. You must dress appropriately as well, dear. Nothing too short or revealing."

"I have the black bell-bottoms and the peach colored top. I'll go and see Carol, she might have another top I can swap over while I wash the peach one."

My mind was racing ahead, getting jumbled with all the things I needed to do before Monday.

"Stacey, I can let you have a few things, my dear. They are probably too old fashioned for your liking, but I do have some pretty blouses that would look good on you, and a skirt or two that should fit well. I'm coming in tomorrow to do some research of my own. I'll bring them in shall I?"

Eunice took a small step backwards ready for me to launch into another hug.

"Thank you." That was all I could manage. My throat was thick with unshed tears. How in the world could I ever thank her adequately for all her kindness?

" I'll only be in for a few hours tomorrow morning, Stacey. Pop up around 9.00 o'clock and you can try the things on in the ladies room. Now, my dear you have a lot to get done. Good luck with finding somewhere to stay. Don't get upset if you can't find anything, we'll work something out, in that eventuality."

I was in a hurry to begin everything, hugging my news to myself and rehearsing in my head how I was going to tell Jamie. I couldn't even begin to think about how I would be able to tell Baby Jenny.

First things first, I headed towards Dulcie's boarding house hoping like hell she had a room available.

I knocked on the door and could hear the dog 'Major' on the other side. "Hold your horses!" Dulcie boomed.

She opened the door and this time I was ready for the dog. After I got the required slurping treatment, I managed to ask about a room.

The room with the porch was taken but the young man in it would be leaving in three weeks time. Dulcie said I could have it then. In the meantime, I could use the couch to sleep on, and use all the facilities. I would pay a reduced rate for that three weeks. For an additional few bucks, she would give me a meal at night and sandwiches for lunch, as I couldn't use the refrigerator to keep my own food in until after the young guy had left.

I didn't care how big she was, I hugged her anyway.

She blushed. I didn't believe it till I saw it. Then she gave me a friendly shove that almost had me in the wall on the other side of the room. Jesus she was big!

What she said next really floored me, "That woman friend of yours, that Eunice at the library, she's real quality, Sassy. She rang me about you, did ya know?"

"What?"

"Yeah, she rang all right. Offered to pay for your room and board till you get ya first pay packet, she did."

"Shit! Did she really? I had no idea. How the hell do I thank her?"

Dulcie thought about the answer for a minute then she just said, "Make it work for you, girl. Make it work and do her proud. You ain't gonna get another chance like this, just don't fuck up."

I gulped the tears back.

"Don't fuck up." She repeated.

"I'll do my damndest to make it work. That is as much as I can promise."

"That should be enough."

The third most pivotal day of my life to date had just taken place. I swore to myself then that nothing would stop me from leaving these streets far behind me. I also swore that I would never forget the people who for no gain to themselves had put themselves out to give me this one shot at a normal life.

The first pivotal day of my life had been on that hot November day back in 1965 when I had taken back my control of my life and walked away from the horrors at 'hell central'.

The second was the day Jamie had found me badly bruised and afraid after being raped and beaten. He and the others had taken me in to the palace, and my life changed forever.

I arranged with Dulcie to come back the next day. I would meet Eunice at the library as arranged and come straight from there to the boarding house.

Tonight though I would spend my last night in the palace. The fourth pivotal moment. I was incredibly sad at the thought of not being with my palace family, yet I knew that for my life to continue and my dreams to stay intact I had to leave.

Tonight I needed to say goodbye to the only people in my life that had ever shown me unconditional love.

It tore at me, and I hovered between what I must do and what I wanted to do. Life is full of 'if only' moments. I knew deep inside of me, that I would be forever saying 'if only' if I didn't at least give myself a chance to see if I could make it in the other world, the world of normal day to day exchanges, the world where the underbelly of life's dark edges was hidden, and denied.

*****

Jamie was sitting alone on the dockside when I got back. He looked up at me and held the look, then he nodded slowly and smiled, "Congratulations, Sass; when do you start?"

"How did you know?"

He shook his head, "You have a way of communicating, it's like sparks come out of those eyes of yours or something. I'm happy for ya, Sassy."

I sat down next to him and remained quiet. I wish I had the words back then, the words to thank him for my life. For had it not been for Jamie I know I would have become just another statistic.

Jamie reached over and took my hand, and I didn't pull away. We sat quietly, communicating silently and just holding each other's hands till it grew dark. It was a union of thought, and a precious moment for us both.

I could hear the others faintly in the distance and knew I couldn't put this off much longer.

Jamie asked me to wait till he got back. He decided to make this a celebration instead of a wake. "Let's make this a party, Sass. Let's laugh and get drunk and bull shit and enjoy tonight. It'll be better, you'll see; leave 'em laughing, you know what I mean."

"But, Jamie ... what do I say to her ... Jenny, what the hell do I tell her? I don't want to tell her, you know that. I'm worried that she'll think I'm abandoning her, you know how unsettled she's been lately."

"Jenny will always feel abandoned, Sass. It's been sort of ingrained in her. No matter what you say or do she's gonna feel that way. So I think we tell Jenny separate from the others. I'll tell her all about my plans to take her with me when I go, before you tell her you're leaving, that way she shouldn't completely freak out. What do you think?"

"Okay ... yeah, yeah that would be better. Thanks, Jamie. For everything."

He didn't respond except to say he'd take Jenny with him when he got the booze and stuff.

He turned away and squeezed my hand tightly. Then he headed off to get some booze and I stayed right where I was till he got back.

He was gone at least an hour and when he came back it was clear that he'd spent a lot of his savings. He hadn't just bought the beer, he'd bought buckets of the new chicken from Kentucky Fried, which had just opened in Sydney.

None of us had ever tried it, and it was a big hit with everyone.

Jenny was even quieter than usual and avoided making eye contact with me. I looked over at Jamie, who was getting into the beer in a big way. I raised my eyebrows and nodded towards Jenny. Had he told her already? He shook his head, no. He walked over to me and whispered, "I told her about my plans to take her with me when I go."

"What did she say?"

"She said she didn't give a fuck what I did."

"Shit. She doesn't mean that, Jamie. She's just lashing out again."

"Yeah, I know. But she's not stupid, Sassy. She knows something big is happening, she's preparing for whatever it is the only way she knows how. Just so you know she's gonna say stuff to you that'll hurt cause it's meant too."

"Jamie, leave it till tomorrow morning. I think I would prefer to tell her away from here. Maybe down at my spot in the gardens. Somewhere she can react the way she needs to without everyone watching."

"You got smarter over the last few years. Yeah ... I agree. Let's just party tonight."

I tried to party, and I got drunk along with everyone else. But my heart wasn't in it. We sang our versions of favourite songs, particularly "Come Together" by The Beatles, our version was R rated. We laughed at nothing and everything; the way we always did when we drank. It was for me the longest night I could remember for a very long time.

Jamie, Jenny, and I went into the gardens early the following morning.

I told her I was leaving the palace.

I waited for the backlash. In many ways I would have preferred her to scream at me, or hit me ...I wanted her to lash out.

Instead, Jenny just stood with her pretty eyes full of tears, and begged me to stay.

Saying no to her was one of the most difficult things I have ever done. But I did it.

I told her I would be living close enough for her and Jamie to come and visit; but I had already decided that I wouldn't come back to the palace.

If they wanted to see me, it would have to be on my new ground. Going back to the palace would never free me to do what I needed to do with my life.

I promised both her and Jamie, that if they decided not to visit me at Dulcie's that I would still see them again. We made a pact, to meet once a year, on the first day of summer, which here in Australia is December 1. We were to meet outside the Opera house, at noon.

We kept that pact. Some years we missed, when our lives took us away to different places for different reasons. But almost every year for the last forty- plus years, at least two of us would arrive. Sometimes as many as five of the old crew would be there.

It was strange and sad and wonderful, to laugh about the old times, and talk about the new.

The morning progressed and the time arrived for Jamie to tell the remainder of the palace gang that I was leaving. I was on the receiving end of some very smelly hugs, and some warm well wishes from the gang. Jenny just held my hand tightly, only letting go when I needed to leave.

I could hear her crying as I walked away.

I will never forget that sound.

I decided it was better to go to the boarding house and leave my ratty bag of clothes before I saw Eunice at the library.

Dulcie was waiting for me when I arrived. She took my one bag and put into a closet she kept under lock and key. We made arrangements about the sheets and towels, which I hadn't even thought about needing and she gave me the rules about guests, and mealtimes, plus a washing up roster for those of her guests that had their meals supplied by her. She showed me the shared laundry and the list of hours for use by each tenant.

The bathroom was shared by the five people boarding there. Four was usually her maximum, she didn't normally allow folks to sleep on the couch, I was so grateful that she had made an exception.

She recommended that I shower at night, when the traffic to the bathroom was light. I had no soap or personal shampoo and products, which she generously provided, saying I could replace them when I was paid.

I hadn't even bothered to ask my new employer about wages, I was simply too excited to have been lucky enough to get the job.

Dulcie gave me my key and hurried me off.

I knew Eunice would be waiting on me arriving at the library and I needed to pick up the pace to be there on time.

I found Eunice sitting outside reading when I arrived, I had no watch, but her glance at her own made me conscious that I had kept her waiting.

"Sorry, Eunice. I should have been here on time; I kinda got caught up at the boarding house."

"The lady that runs the place seems very pleasant, Stacey. You should be happy there."

"Thank you for offering to pay my first weeks board, Eunice. That was very very kind of you. I will pay you back when I get paid."

"You won't be able to do it all in one hit, dear, remember you will need to budget your wages to cover all your personal needs."

"I have been getting by with no money at all, for a long time now. So anything left over would be an improvement."

"You may find that you need more things in your life now, my dear. Just have a good think about what you spend your money on, and you should get by nicely. I have those few clothes I mentioned for you. Come along and you can try them on in the ladies room."

We headed into the sanctity of the library and she handed me two plastic bags, both of them packed full.

The clothes looked brand new to me, they had that feel to them and that certain smell that all unworn things seem to have.

There were two skirts, a little longer than I would normally have worn, but they fit really well. I can't recall how many pretty blouses were in the other bag, but they were lovely, a little older in style than the current stuff I saw being worn, but I was utterly thrilled with them. I would have more than enough to see me through till I could buy some stuff of my own. I made a mental note to get some laundry powder as a priority.

Eunice checked me out with each change of clothes and was clearly delighted with what she had given me.

We agreed that I would come and meet her after work on payday to settle up a portion of the money that she was paying Dulcie on my behalf.

She handed me an envelope with one week's board and food money in it to give to Dulcie .

"I have no idea when payday is, I should've asked all sorts of stuff, but I guess I was a little excited at getting the job. Can I phone you when I know what day I get paid, and what hours I'm supposed to be working? That way I can come up here and meet you after I finish for the day."

"That would be ideal, my dear." She walked over to her work station and wrote two numbers down for me. One being the library and the other was her home telephone number in case of 'emergencies' she said.

"Are you nervous about Monday, dear?"

"Nervous? Who me? Nyah … I'm not nervous Eunice, I'm bloody terrified."

She laughed and gave me a pat on the arm, "Just be yourself, Stacey. You will find people are more than willing to treat you well, if you do the same to them."

"Yeah?"

"Yes."

"I guess I'll just need to be quiet and watch my mouth."

"Don't ever be afraid to ask questions about what you are doing, dear. People would rather you ask questions than make mistakes. Remember that, also remember that your employer will allow for questions and errors, especially during the first few weeks."

"I don't know how I can thank you for all you have done, Eunice. I mean everything. Right from that first day when you showed me Vietnam and Australia and all those other places on the world globe. Remember when I thought Vietnam was in America someplace?"

"Yes, dear. I remember it well. I also recall that you were amazed that the earth was round and how … what was it you said, 'How come we don't fall off the bottom?'"

I laughed and felt my face turning red at the memory. I knew absolutely nothing about anything normal, but could've had a master's degree in life back then.

Eunice and I exchanged laughs about my earlier self. I had learned so much here in the library, and not just book learning, I also learned that there were some really decent 'straight' people in the world. I had been lucky enough to meet more than one of them.

Eunice was special and I gave her the closest thing I could manage to a hug.

She smiled at me and wished me luck for my first day at work. She asked if I had time and access to a telephone at the boarding house if I could give her a call and let her know how I was doing at work.

I left clutching my bags of goodies and the envelope for Dulcie tucked neatly into my knife sheath.

I recall wondering how I could conceal my flick-knife under my new clothes.

So much for my attitude of gratitude.

I was about as unprepared for this new experience as it gets.

Chapter 19

I didn't sleep well on the Sunday night.

Although the couch was incredibly comfortable.

After the floors I had been used to for so long it felt like the height of luxury to me. I had slept okay on the Saturday night, once I got accustomed to being warm and comfortable.

But Sunday wouldn't let me rest. I had eaten a home cooked meal for the first time I could ever remember and it was just so delicious. There seemed to be so much of it, and then we had Ice cream and fruit salad. I couldn't get over just how big the servings were, and I was tempted to divide it in half and save some for the next day. Old habits die hard, to this day, I save all my leftovers. I have never quite gotten over the memory of being hungry and having nothing to eat.

I still eat like there is no tomorrow. Because my memory recalls a time when tomorrow was always in doubt. I have never been able to gain weight though.

I was showered and dressed by 6.00 am. Dulcie had given me some deodorant, which I'd never heard of. Who knew that you could buy stuff to make you smell nice? To add to the feeling she also squirted me with some perfume. It was a little overpowering but a hell of a lot better than the aroma I normally had.

I arrived for work at 8.00 am on the dot, with sandwiches provided by Dulcie in a plastic container.

Mrs. O'Keefe was smiling as I walked in after knocking on her door.

"Good morning, Stacey. You look very nice this morning. Please take a seat, and I will just go over some of the conditions of employment with you.

I wish I could recall that entire conversation, it was important … I was so nervous I felt sick to my stomach. I vaguely heard her describe what I would be learning to do. I was amazed at the wages, which seemed huge to me, but were in fact lower than the average wage, and less than half of what males were paid doing the same job. Equal pay for equal work was still a long way off.

"The Female Eunuch" by Germaine Greer was released that year if memory serves me correctly. Eunice gave me a copy of it with hand written notes she had made and placed throughout the book explaining the terminology and several other things I had no idea about.

Mrs. O'Keefe introduced me to the remaining staff that I would be working directly with, and then I met Laurie, who would be training me.

She was a softly spoken and work dedicated woman, and thankfully, she had a kind and patient manner. I must have driven her mad with questions that first few weeks.

She showed me how the files were laid out, and allocated me a desk where I could sort things alphabetically before starting the filing. That was to be my first task every morning.

The switchboard looked terrifyingly complicated to me. It was not like the systems they have now. This thing belonged in the Ark. Plugs and holes to put them in. I must have cut so many people off especially in that first few days. Poor Mrs. O'Keefe must have wondered what the hell she'd done hiring me, as the complaints came in about waiting on forever and then being disconnected.

Like everything else I have ever learned there comes a time when suddenly the penny drops and it all makes sense. After an hour a day for the first week, that's what happened, and then I began looking forward to relieving on the switchboard during the lunch breaks. I felt very sophisticated and oh so important! I had also begun to speak differently, without saying fuck or cool every second word. The fuck word slipped out when I was nervous or agitated, and I could almost hear the gasps of shock from anyone overhearing me.

I learned quickly to say "far out" instead. Thank you John Denver.

I was meant to take my lunch hour from eleven to twelve, most of the time in that first month I forgot to take it at all, and often ate my sandwiches on the way back to the boarding house.

I loved the job. I loved living in the boarding house. In fact I couldn't remember a time when I'd ever felt so content with my life.

The guy in the room I wanted moved out as expected, and I had a bedroom that was my space only. My room. My porch. I discovered that I am an extremely territorial female. I don't have any idea if that was just me or a result of being constantly on alert my whole life to danger approaching.

I still wore my knife every day, under my acceptable and very uncontroversial clothes. It remained strapped around my waist, and disguised by wearing one of the pretty tops that Eunice and Carol had given me.

I would get home just before six each evening and go straight to my room. The shower was mine for half an hour, and I used every second of that time, luxuriating in being clean.

Dulcie would have dinner served at 7.30 promptly each evening. The people in the boarding house changed quite often. Norman was in the room next to mine and he was a sweet man. He was also working as an entertainer and slept during the day. I found his humor wonderful, and he had an eye for color and fashion that he was happy to share. He worked as a female impersonator at a club in Kings Cross and if I needed makeup or my nails done Norman was always delighted to help me out.

Norman and I were often the only ones sitting down to dinner at night, and I rarely saw him during the day. The others had different hours and different needs, and I would normally only see them in the shared laundry or on their way in and out of the boarding house.

Dulcie had a room with a television and a radio in it that we used, and we often had her company at night, especially if there were a good movie on. The dog would lay at her feet, and we would all sit and smoke and relax as we watched.

I had taken to meeting Eunice for a coffee on Friday evenings after work. That was usually the only evening I didn't have dinner at the boarding house. We would chat and catch up on each other's week. I had paid Eunice back slowly over the first month at her insistence. She was a wise woman, and made certain I knew how to budget my small salary carefully. I so enjoyed her company. Once every month or two we would go to a movie together, with me choosing one month and her the next. I felt almost normal. I was doing some of the everyday things that I heard the others at work talking about.

They were a friendly group of people, however I refused any invitations to mix with the younger ones after hours. Occasionally if someone I liked had a birthday, I would go to the pub for a drink after work, and buy them a drink. Apart from that, I steered clear of socializing with them. I felt it a wiser move than being expected to answer any casual questions about my life.

I simply would not allow my past to dirty up my present.

Chapter 20

I had been working in the office for around a year or so when I was promoted to the front counter.

I was so thrilled to be given the responsibility of interviewing folks that wanted to open a store account. I had learned to speak reasonably properly or at least without dropping the "F" bomb in company.

Applying for a credit account was simple back then. Basic stuff like employment, home address, three references etc: this was in the days long before credit cards were the normal mode of purchase. Credit cards weren't issued then, an individual contract was drawn up for each purchase.

A young guy came in to buy some tires for his car, on hire purchase.

He worked in a bank, lived at home with his folks, and was the best-looking male I had ever seen.

I acknowledged that to myself. It didn't make me feel any different, it was more like looking at a painting and recognizing that the artist had done a damned fine job. His name was Jeff.

His account was referenced and approved. I had the job of notifying him by telephone that he was free to come and pick up his goods.

Jeff was pleased.

Three days later, he came back in and asked me on a date.

It appears that friends of his were leaving on a world cruise and they had asked him to a cocktail party on board ship the night before they were to sail. I was surprised by the invitation, and curious having never been on a luxury cruise ship...or to a cocktail party (whatever the hell that was.)

I had no idea. The idea that they were cruising around the world was enough to leave me speechless. I had only read about folks with the money to do that sort of thing.

I asked some of the older ladies at work what to wear to a "Cocktail Party"

They certainly enjoyed setting me straight on what's why's and wherefores. I felt incredibly intimidated learning that most females who attended this sort of thing would be dressed in Cocktail dresses. Apparently very expensive items.

Only the wealthy normally threw and attended such things I was warned.

Well I figured that must be wrong. My date couldn't be wealthy and need to buy tires on credit.

He wasn't wealthy by most standards of such things, he did come from a comfortably off family, with a large home in a fine area. His folks could easily have afforded the tires for instance, but they liked and encouraged him to accept some responsibilities on his own. Hence the job and the credit.

I borrowed a black skirt from one of the women at work, and a white frilly blouse from another. I washed my hair and wore it up in a bun. That was the best I could manage.

I felt underdressed and way out of my depth when we arrived.

I was introduced to the couple going on the cruise, they seemed friendly enough and curious about me by the number of questions I was asked. I left that conversation as quickly as I could.

Luckily, most of the guests just gave me a disinterested glance and chatted to their friends.

Jeff didn't look comfortable either. He confided that he'd felt obligated to come as the guy going on the cruise was one of the senior members of the bank where he worked.

We escaped and headed outside on the top deck and sat in the warm night air, with the drift of music from the main dining room wafting up to us on the breeze.

It was a simply beautiful night … and I couldn't wait for it to end.

I hated feeling so out of my depth. I wasn't about to start acting any different to try and fit in either. Too easy to get caught out doing that silly shit.

We sat and had a few drinks and then I asked him to take me home.

He dropped me at the boarding house and before he left he asked me if he could make up for a boring evening by taking me someplace of my choice the next day. I was interested and it would be a Sunday so I would have spent the time doing my laundry or something just as exciting.

Although I couldn't understand why he would be bothered at all, so I asked him.

He surprised me by saying that I was different to the girls he usually dated (Brother what an understatement!} he found me interesting and he thought we could have some fun together.

The few dates I had ever been on had been unmitigated disasters. As soon as the guys got touchy feely I ran like hell.

I accepted his offer and suggested we go to Manly beach for the day. He seemed pleased and we arranged to leave early to make the most of the glorious summer weather.

He arrived right on time, and I was so much more comfortable wearing jeans with my one-piece costume underneath.

He had a picnic hamper packed and we set off with the radio blaring. I enjoyed the drive with the top down and the fresh wind in my hair.

Manly is such a lovely spot, we found some shade under the Norfolk Island Pines that ring the beach. He put down a blanket on the grass area, and we sat and unpacked the hamper. I got excited when he lifted out the king prawns. I adore seafood, but it was way beyond my price range.

He was relaxed and that helped me do the same. We chatted and soon found ourselves laughing over things we both enjoyed or found funny. He was so easy to be with; I didn't feel threatened. Which was unusual in itself. The few dates I had been on had been disastrous with me being super defensive, and my mouth getting me into no end of trouble.

Jeff seemed gentle. His whole demeanor was comfortable and easy going.

We had a wonderful day, with much laughter shared as we splashed each other in the water then floated around without a care in the world. I felt almost normal, looking around at the other teenagers on the beach. For the first time I didn't feel like I had a label attached that people could see.

I had felt up to that point that I stood out from others my age, as if they could see the horror of my past just by looking at me. I know that is ridiculous, but at the time my insecurity in social situations had me being aggressive and abrasive.

I wanted so badly to belong and had no way of knowing how the hell to do it.

Jeff dropped me at home, and asked if he could call me during the week.

I said okay. I didn't expect him to call. I was shocked when he did, and pleased. We went to the movies, 'Easy rider' had been released the year before and I wanted badly to see it. We both loved it, and the music.

Jack Nicholson is still one of my all time favorite actors.

Jeff again dropped me home. He made no attempt at physical contact. I was so grateful for that.

Jeff and I saw each other almost every night for the next 3 weeks. He would give me a gentle kiss on the lips when it was time to leave and never put any hard moves on me.

We sat out on my porch in the boarding house one night shortly after the 3 weeks was up. We weren't talking much, just sitting sipping on a beer and relaxing.

Jeff reached over and took my hand, "Stacey; will you marry me?"

"Pardon?" I squeaked.

He laughed, "You heard me. Will you marry me?"

I was utterly dumbfounded. "Marry you? Why, I mean, why would you want to do that?"

"Because I love you." he said

"Shit!"

"Well that's not what I was hoping you'd say." He was smiling.

"Oh…hell, I mean no… not hell, but … you don't know me! I mean you do kind of, but not really."

"I like what I see, Stace. I'm in love with you. Maybe I should have waited, but I'm worried someone else will come along and I'll lose you."

"Jeff, you don't know anything about me, really. There is stuff…some stuff that…"

"It doesn't matter. Whatever it is … it doesn't matter. Can you think about it…please? Don't give me an answer yet. Okay? Think about it…please, I will ask you again in a week. Just think about it. I will look after you always. Think about that too, okay?"

"Okay…I will, think I mean. Thank you for asking me. No matter what I decide, okay. I'm just blown away, that you asked."

"I'll go now. Can I call you tomorrow? I'll just call, all right. I won't come over till you have had a chance to think."

"Okay…yes…call me."

He left then.

My head was spinning.

I had no idea what to do.

I took a few days off work, calling in sick with flu. I needed to think this through and not knee jerk react as I normally did with everything.

I was afraid.

 I liked, Jeff a lot. But was that enough?

 I doubted I could fall in love in the way I'd heard it could be.

I had no illusions about male and female relationships, having witnessed the worst of them so very young. I was damaged goods. I knew it. Would it be fair to marry Jeff without him knowing about my past?

 Yet if I told him…what then?

I was certain he would run like hell.

I could be a good wife, I was sure of that. But what about the physical stuff?

What would I do about the fact that I loved being cuddled but hated the very thought of sex?

I didn't sleep. I couldn't. I hovered around the question in my mind for days.

Would I be able to be a real wife to Jeff, in every way? Could I go into this knowing that my ability to respond physically was zero? Unless I faked it, which is all I had ever been taught to do. But this wasn't one of the clients back in hell central. This was a decent and caring young man.

I was so confused.

A big part of me wanted this so badly. He had spoken about his family with such love in his voice. He had a normal family. According to him, his mother and father had been together over 30 years. They didn't drink or smoke. They did everything together including family holidays with him and his older married brother.

A family…a family that was normal. A family I could belong to, and be proud of. Oh dear lord; I wanted that so much. I wanted a mom I could talk to about female stuff. I had never known what it was like to have a father either. I mean a real one.

Jeff had uncles and aunts and cousins that all appeared to be close as well.

The temptation to say yes was huge.

But the fact that I would need to have sex…would be expected to have sex regularly…That terrified me.

I wanted to belong to a family. I wanted to have Mother's Days and Father's Days and Easter, Christmas and birthdays with a family I belonged to.

I wanted it so bad I could taste it.

Could I be a wife to Jeff? Could I make him happy that he had chosen me as his life partner?

Did I have the right to go into the marriage ceremony knowing that I was in all probability going to have to fake the sexual aspect of the relationship?

I didn't sleep for three days. Trying to weigh up what I could give to the marriage and what I may never be able to give.

I spoke with him on the telephone a couple of times. He was patient with me, but clearly wanted an answer and soon.

The week was up, and he was coming around to see me and expected an answer.

I had decided to say no.

He arrived on time as always and we sat out on the porch.

I felt ill. My nerves were in scrambled egg mode.

Jeff was very quiet for a while, and then he said quietly, "its no, isn't it? No, don't say anything yet, okay. Hear me out. He shifted and turned around completely to face me and took my hand in his, "I will never expect you to do anything you aren't happy with, Stacey. You have mentioned a few times now that you have stuff … bad stuff in your past. I want you to know I don't care about that, whatever it is. If you want to tell me that's fine, but I promise you I will never ask. Do you love me?"

Oh … hell. What could I say…I searched for words that wouldn't hurt him, "I love you as a person, Jeff. I think it's love … but I don't think I'm *in* love with you. I'm not sure what being in love means exactly, but I care enough about you not to want to put you in a place that may end up hurting you badly. I'm so afraid that I will cause you to be hurt. Can you understand that? Please."

He nodded, "I think I can understand. But a lot of people get married for bad reasons; we at least would start as friends. We are friends, I think."

"Is that enough? Being friends, I mean. Marriage is more than just friendship, Jeff. At least I believe you need more than that."

"We could face any obstacles if we had to. I know we could."

My head was saying No, no, no don't. My need to finally be part of something good said yes.

"Can we take it slow? If I say yes...*If* I do, I would want to wait a year. I would need that time to really get to know you, and you definitely need to know me better. I am damaged Jeff. I simply don't know how much of that dark stuff will affect us."

"So ...yes? If we get engaged for a year? Are you saying that?"

I nodded. My head was spinning and I felt sick in the gut. "Okay, yes...yes Jeff, but at least a year. Undertood?"

"You won't be sorry, Stacey." He leaned over and kissed me gently. "I'll make certain you don't regret it."

He asked me if he needed to ask for my hand, to get my parent's permission. I laughed. Then I recall saying, "They are dead to me, Jeff. Not technically dead, but dead nonetheless. I don't ever want to see them again."

He looked stunned. "But, Stace, they're your parents, surely you want them to know, and to meet me, don't you?"

I almost changed my mind right there and then.

He caught the look on my face, "Are they part of the damage?"

"They caused the damage; well the woman that gave birth to me did; I've never met my father." I said stiffly. I want to wait until I don't need parental consent to marry you. That woman … is dead to me."

"I'll never mention them again, I promise. What do you want to tell my folks, about your family?"

"Tell them I'm an orphan. Tell them I have no idea who my family was, please, Jeff."

"What if they ask if you were ever adopted?"

"Tell them no. That's all, just no."

"Okay. Okay, I guess they'll believe that. They're very old-fashioned. I don't know how they'll react, Stace."

"Believe me, Jeff. The truth would devastate them. If we are going to have a good chance at the marriage thing, this is the only way I can do it."

He looked confused and then shook his head, "Surely nothing could be as bad as all that?"

My throat went dry. "It's up to you. I will tell you everything and then you can walk away if you want to, okay?"

"No. No, I don't want to know. You are here and I love you, that's enough."

I believed him. Because I wanted to so very badly.

Two weeks later, I was wearing a beautiful solitaire diamond ring.

That was the night he took me home to meet his family.

*****

We drove through the city and across the Harbor Bridge. Apparently, Jeff's family lived on the North Shore. It was one of the most affluent suburbs of Sydney.

The house was large, but not a mansion…it was set back amongst the trees on a block of land that was enormous, to my city girl way of thinking.

"What have you told them, about me I mean?" I asked.

"Nothing, well your name, and that's about it. They know we have been seeing each other for a while."

"What did they say about us being engaged?"

"I haven't told them yet."

"WHAT?"

"I wanted them to meet you, I'll tell them tonight. It will be fine, Stacey."

"Oh. That's great! Hi Mom and Dad this is Stacey nobody from nowhere and she's going to be your daughter-in-law. Sure … they'll be just delighted. I can't believe you didn't prepare them. They'll hate me…I know it." My insecurity was working overtime, I wanted to cut and run like hell.

Jeff insisted it would be all right. He took my hand and we climbed out of the car and walked the long steep path up to the house.

I learned very quickly that Jeff would always avoid emotional scenes. He couldn't cope with them. That was just the way he'd been raised.

His folks were sitting on the sofa holding hands when we breezed in. I knew they weren't expecting company so the handholding was no act. I was stunned to say the least. I felt like I'd walked into the set of 'Leave it to Beaver' or something.

I had nothing to compare to that evening. Jeff's Mom and Dad were welcoming and kind. I was no threat to their youngest Son after all.

They managed to remain kind even after Jeff told them we were going to be married. His Mom went so pale I was certain she would faint. His dad looked worriedly from one of us to the other…"You're both very young." He cleared his throat. "Marriage is a very big step." He looked at his wife and back at us, "Do you need to get married?" he asked in a whisper.

"No … no we don't. I'm sorry this is a big shock to you. I think we could have handled it better. We will be engaged for a year at least, to be certain that we know each other, um…properly." I responded…wishing I could vanish through the Persian carpet at my feet.

They seemed to breathe in unison. "That's sensible. Very sensible. We look forward to getting to know you, young woman." His dad said. His mom still looked shocked…but at least her color was a little better.

"Well, Son. I think we should have a get together to er celebrate your engagement. It will give your young lady a chance to meet the whole family, and we of course will have a chance to meet hers."

I felt like I had been asked to produce pedigree papers.

 I was wrong. They weren't like that at all. They were and remained the most loving and supportive people I had ever or will ever know.

Jeff was itching to leave; he looked trapped. He glanced worriedly at his Mom who was still silent. He turned to me and suggested we leave. "If your parents don't mind." I said.

"Of course not, my dear." Said his Mother.

"We will have you over for dinner and a small get together in a week or so, would that suite you, er…Stacey?" she continued politely.

I recall saying 'Thank you, yes". I stood awkwardly not knowing what the hell to do.

Jeff's Dad put his hand out and I shook it. His Mom looked uncertain, but then stood and gave me a brief stiff hug.

"Well good night and um … Thank you." I muttered

Jeff said, "I'll be back later."

And we left.

*****

I didn't speak in the car as Jeff drove me back to the boarding house. I was trying to sort the evening out in my head.

Jeff made polite conversation about nothing at all. He was clearly worried.

"It was pretty damned unfair, doing that…to them and to me, Jeff. Why didn't you at least tell me that they didn't know, about our engagement I mean?"

"I thought you'd break it off with me if I did." He muttered the words.

"I probably would have. So what the hell did you tell them about my background?"

"Nothing, not yet. They didn't ask accept for where did I meet you, and I told them about your job and the tires and stuff. That's all they know."

"Yeah, well you don't know a hell of a lot beyond that yourself, do you?"

"It doesn't make any difference, Stacey. I told you. You aren't marrying them, you're marrying me." That appeared to be the end of that conversation.

******

The dinner and small get together went reasonably well. There were a few awkward moments when one of Jeff's Aunts asked me where I had grown up.

Jeff's Mom rescued me, "Oh, Stacey has lived all over Sydney, Jean. She has grown up in Foster homes. Haven't you, my dear?" she said with her hand gently resting on my shoulder.

Her manner and stance indicated that that was the end of that conversation. Jeff's Aunt smiled and said, "How unfortunate. I am sorry, my dear."

I gave my future mother-in-law a grateful smile, and she squeezed my shoulder in response. There was a lot more to this woman than appeared on the surface. I soon discovered to my joy, that for her, family was everything. How I longed to be a part of that.

The men headed towards the large sitting room to watch the cricket. The women including me began clearing the tables that had been set so beautifully.

"Stacey … we, that is the family, we don't know what you would like as engagement gifts. Can you give us some ideas? Or do you have a gift book in David Jones?" This from my future sister-in-law, Jane. She was very stiff and formal but she seemed okay.

"David Jones?" I had never been game enough to go in there even to just look. The windows were filled with beautiful things with price tags that would have equaled a year's worth of my salary plus more.

"I uh…I haven't given it a lot of thought, not yet. I'll ask Jeff what he thinks."

"Jeff! Good heavens, Pet; you will end up with a room full of science fiction books." His Mom was laughing at the very idea. That did it; I started laughing. Then I got the hic ups.

She gave me a warm hug. "We girls will chat about it later, how would that be?"

I knew then that I had been accepted. Rightly or wrongly, they were going to be my family. I felt so much joy at the thought of it; I managed to quash all the negative thoughts that had plagued me about the rightness of marrying Jeff.

I had never met anyone like his parents before.

If I were to write a one-word definition of Jeff's mother, it would be Lady…with a large capital L. She epitomized that word for me.

She was regal in bearing, fiercely protective of her family, gentle, sweet and elegance personified, I came to learn she also had a wonderful warm sense of humor and took great pleasure in caring for her beautiful home. She taught me more than anyone else in my life how to be feminine without being a wimp.

As for Jeff's dad, he was a marvelous character, with his slightly dark humor, intense loyalty to the country he had fought for, dedication to business, and unrelenting love for all his family. I respected him in a way I had never respected any other male in my short life.

I came to them with nothing…they gifted me with unconditional love.

Everything else was pure bonus.

Chapter 21

I had been lucky so far. Since Jeff and I became engaged, I hadn't had that dreadful pain. I'd hoped that it was gone.

It hit me late on a Saturday afternoon whilst Jeff and I were clearing up after a barbecue at his folks place.

It hit hard and very fast. I went down in a heap.

I couldn't complain and beg not to go to hospital, not anymore. I had to get over that mountain and allow my future family the opportunity to take care of me.

I had been asked to call the folks Mom and Dad. It was a real pleasure.

Dad placed me gently in the car, and drove me to the emergency room at the hospital, which was only 5 minutes from their home. I tried to reassure them that it would be okay, that I'd had it before, but I was in too much pain to make much sense.

Mom sat on one side of the bed holding tightly to my hand. Jeff couldn't cope seeing me in pain, so his father took him outside for a smoke.

The nurses took my vital signs and hurried off. A doctor was with me within minutes.

He spoke quietly to Jeff's mom. Then she left after squeezing my hand and telling me she'd be on the other side of the curtain.

The doctor seemed kind, he apologized that he had to press down on my abdomen, but he needed to check some things. He pressed and I screamed.

He patted my shoulder and said how sorry he was, and that he would give me something for the pain. I expected aspirin…I got morphine. It slowed the pain to just a nasty ache. I was so grateful for that, I hadn't believed the pain could ever be eased by anything.

Jeff and his parents came back in for a short while. The doctor asked me how I was doing since the injection. I thanked him, and said the pain was still there, but not so bad. He checked my blood pressure and frowned. The nurse was called and she came back with another injection of morphine…that one really hit the spot. I floated in and out of sleep for hours.

When I awoke properly, I was alone. I felt very nauseated and began vomiting. I didn't know about the buzzer to call the nurse.

The sister came hurrying in when she heard me being ill. I thought I'd get into serious shit having thrown up everywhere. She just shook her head and bustled off to get the junior nurses to change the bedding and me.

I continued being sick into the bowl provided. The sister was kind. She washed my face and hands and freshened my bowl, saying that she had rung for the doctor to come back and give me something for the vomiting. The same Doctor came in; he spoke to her quietly and then took a seat next to my bed and explained that I would be staying in hospital for tests for a day or so. He wanted to ascertain what was causing the pain of course and he had a mile of questions about it, and my history with it.

He seemed angry when I told him I hadn't gone to a hospital or doctor about it before. I asked him if he had to tell anyone what I told him. He said a very definite no.

I gave him no details other than I had had an "accident" when I was very young and I had been getting the pain regularly ever since.

He pushed for more information; I wouldn't give away the kids back at the Palace. He had to be content with me saying that I came from a less than terrific background. That was it. End of discussion. I was older but no more trusting, and sadly still terrified of Gwen being able to find me.

He couldn't give me an answer without tests being done about what had caused the pain. He queried my diet, he asked if I was a heavy drinker, and he left and came back with another injection of morphine with an added hit of maxalon… to counteract the vomiting.

He inserted a cannula in my hand and said that they would put up saline to keep me hydrated.

I was taken up to the ward.

The pain hit full force again several hours later. I was worried about pushing the button for a nurse; I didn't want to make waves. So I stupidly lay there until I was curled up in bloody agony again. I was angry with myself. I was afraid and I was determined to get out of there and go back to my room in the boarding house.

I didn't realize I was moaning out loud. One of the other patients in the four-bed ward rang for the nurse.

The sister came and checked my chart, and my BP and temperature. She left and came back with a bowl of tepid water and bathed my face.

A different doctor on duty and he was much older than the one I'd seen earlier.

He drew more blood. Then he wrote on my chart, and I was given yet another shot of morphine. It must have been a large dose. It knocked me out.

When I came around again I had been moved. I later learned I was in intensive care.

That was the beginning of a lifetime of hospitalizations. A lifetime of being given narcotics to battle a pain they couldn't find a way of stopping.

Every time the pain hit I remembered what had caused it. A vicious circle that spun me out of control. Every time the pain hit...I was mentally back in 'hell central.'

*****

Jeff's friends became my friends. They were a nice bunch of normal healthy teenagers. They loved music, getting stoned and just hanging out.

I felt like a senior citizen when I listened to them bitching about their lives at home, and smiled as they discussed what they were going to do when they got places of their own. It was like being in the company of Aliens. But they were harmless and very likeable Aliens and they welcomed me to the group without question.

The year of our engagement flew by.

It was an intense time for Jeff and me. He continued to be gentle, yet his physical needs were obvious when we alone together.

The need to consummate our relationship was becoming an uncomfortable reminder that I couldn't avoid much longer. I knew it would be soon. I didn't have any idea if I could carry it off without shutting down. I also knew I couldn't marry Jeff without knowing I could handle the sexual side of our relationship without totally flipping out.

Jeff's folks were just amazing. Mom had taken me to her heart and she and I developed a warm and mutually supportive and loving relationship. She looked at me from time to time with a question on her face, yet she never stepped over that invisible line.

I had absolutely no idea how to cook. My experience thus far had been boiling water and vegetables.

I confided my concerns to Mom. She looked at me in amazement, the thought that a young woman of my age had no concept of how to buy and prepare food was beyond her comprehension. She took it upon herself to teach me…she laughed frequently about not wanting to have Jeff hanging around all the time waiting for a meal.

I learned well apparently. Although she was a good cook, her best skills were mainly in the area of cakes, and biscuits. The main meals were all very plain and her best dish was roast lamb, chicken or pork. Nothing fancy. I was the one who was amazed that neither she nor dad had ever had take away food. They had never experienced Chinese food. They had never eaten Pizza!

I took it upon myself to broaden their culinary experiences with memorable moments over the years. I still remember the day on one of our many trips away together when dad proudly ordered 4 cups of chino. The waiter looked confused as hell… Jeff didn't rescue his father, so I did…I looked at the waiter and grinned. "Cappuccino…Yes."

The waiter smiled at Dad, thinking he had been pulling his leg.

I wasn't all that surprised to learn that their trips to Europe had them eating Chicken Schnitzel nearly everywhere they went.

 To the best of my knowledge, they had never eaten French or Italian food…even when in Rome and Paris.

****

The wedding date was approaching fast and I was still avoiding the issue of intimacy. When it was only a couple of months away I knew that I had to make a decision and very soon.

I promised myself that I would do what was right in this situation, if I shutdown completely on Jeff, then I had decided to end our engagement. I wouldn't and couldn't marry him if I was unable to satisfy myself that I could make him happy in that area of our relationship.

I think about it now with 20/20 hindsight, knowing that I will always regret that I wasn't more open with him. The rest of our marriage was wonderful, but it was never enough to counteract my lack of enthusiasm in the bedroom. I could satisfy my husband, but I could never enthusiastically initiate physical contact.

Jeff was a gentle and considerate lover. I was able to tolerate being physical without shutting down on him. I hoped that would be enough.

Chapter 22

Our Wedding day dawned clear and crisp.

My gown was beautiful. I had never worn anything so lovely. I felt like royalty as I walked down that aisle on the arm of Jeff's father.

Our mutual friends sat on my side of the church so it didn't appear empty.

I had invited Jamie and Jenny to the wedding, but I knew they wouldn't come. We had promised that we would never let our separate worlds collide with the days in the palace.

My nerves were shot. I could feel my bouquet of yellow roses shaking as I walked.

Jeff's folks had paid for everything. Jeff and his groomsmen and best man wore top hat and tails

I will not go into detail about our physical relationship. I respect Jeff and his privacy too much for that.

I will say that it wasn't as he or I hoped it would be.

I simply couldn't respond naturally. I was on autopilot. I responded with my body, but not my emotions.

I felt inadequate… and he blamed himself and his inexperience. The sadness of that still lingers for me. He deserved much more. He settled for so much less.

Our affection stayed intact. I craved it. I needed the warmth. The time we shared together outside the bedroom was loving and for me just wonderful.

I belonged now. I had a family.

Had I believed in a God I would have prayed that my life would stay, as it was right then.

I will share some of the moments of our years together with you. We were together for 27 years, and most of those years were happy. The tinges of sadness, and worry about my failing health were always present; but for me at least the rest of it was good.

*****

Let me share with you my first experience at cooking for my new husband.

I had decided to cook a Chinese meal, something really special.

I had the recipe for Mongolian lamb, had all the ingredients bought, and ready.

I would accompany it with a fried rice dish.

The Mongolian lamb went well; it took an absolute age to prepare but tasted okay.

The fried rice was an absolute disaster. Who knew that you were supposed to boil it first? It was called fried rice!

So that's exactly what I did. Raw rice into hot sesame oil. It didn't look right to me, and it certainly didn't taste right, but Jeff crunched his way through it as if it were the best he'd ever had.

I'm amazed I didn't kill him with my attempts at cooking exotic food. He was made of sturdy stuff all right.

*****

We had discussed having children, and had both decided to wait until we were ready, we wanted to travel, and Jeff wanted to be earning enough for me to be able to stop working.

My constant bouts of ill health and the hospitalizations that occurred as a result took a heavy toll.

Jeff's job took us overseas. We lived in New Guinea for several years.

I was at work the day before Anzac Day in 1978. I had been feeling vaguely unwell…not with the pain I was accustomed to. This was different. I went into the rest rooms thinking my period must be due as I was experiencing severe cramping pains.

The amount of blood loss was far more than normal.

I left the rest rooms and went over to my friend Marie's desk. She gave me a smile then took another look at my face, "What the hell! Stacey, you're as white as a ghost! What's wrong?"

"I don't know, hon. But I think I need to get to a hospital."

The ambulance arrived very quickly, and I was taken to the nearest hospital.

I was in the operating theatre very soon after arrival.

I was pregnant. Sadly, it was an ectopic pregnancy (Which I had never heard of). The poor little baby had begun to grow in my left fallopian tube. The tube had ruptured.

The surgeon took the tube to stop me hemorrhaging.

Jeff arrived very quickly; he was sitting by the bed when I came around. We both cried.

The surgeon told us that the chances of me conceiving and carrying a baby were remote.

Apparently, my insides were badly damaged by scar tissue.

Jeff didn't ask questions.

The surgeon asked me later when Jeff had gone home what had caused the internal damage. I choked up. I wanted to tell him, but by the look on his face, he already knew. He patted my hand, "I'm so very sorry my dear. I wish I could offer you a solution. Your husband doesn't know what caused the damage …does he?"

I shook my head, then I rolled over on my side to block out the thoughts chasing around in my mind. When would my damned past stop causing damage to my life?

Was having a shot at happiness too much to ask?

The doctor came in at the sister's request. I was sedated and permitted no visitors until the next day.

Chapter 23

I kept my promise to meet the palace crew on the first day of summer, every year that I was back home in Australia, and not in hospital.

It was always a funny, sad and emotional time. Catching up with them was a mixture always of sadness and laughter.

We would eat and drink, laugh, cry and drink even more. Always reluctant to leave each other's company…always aware that each time together could be our last.

Cassie and Flyman had both died in the first five years after the 'palace' was abandoned.

I can still see Cassie, with her pretty smile and track marked arms.

She fought hard to stay clean, away from the deadly lure of heroin and the things she had to do in order to keep the memory-destroying drug in her system. It was soul destroying, yet her soul in so many ways was already dead.

She tried, please believe that. She tried so damned hard…and she had times when she succeeded for months at a time...

Then something or someone would trigger her demons…and no matter what any of us did or said, we knew she would be gone again.

Jamie was still in touch with a lot of people back on the streets of Kings Cross. It was he that learned of her death.

She died of an overdose, slumped in a filthy toilet with the needle still stuck in her vein.

She was just twenty years old.

Was it deliberate? I don't know…and I don't care. She was a dear sweet young woman, pretty, intelligent and with a wealth of love inside her to share.

She never saw herself that way.

I still see her laughing, I still hear her singing along to the radio, I still feel her gentle touch as she cut my hair with a pair of blunt scissors, expressing her dream to one day own her own Salon…She was going to name it Cassie's Cuts.

She never had the chance.

*****

The Flyman…was eighteen. He wanted to join the army. He wanted to go to Vietnam and represent his country. He was tall, gangly and redheaded, with a temper that went right along with it.

He was so excited the day he scrubbed up and went off to enlist in the Army.

He was anxious that he wouldn't be accepted. He wasn't sure they would take him with no education to speak of, he could read…and he could write; he hoped that would be enough.

He didn't know where Vietnam was…and he didn't care. He just wanted to wear the uniform and belong to a group of people that fought for something real.

The army said no. We never found out why.

The Flyman went a little crazy. He began drinking heavily. He got himself beaten up and thrown in jail regularly. Jamie said he would deliberately pick fights he could never win.

Joining the Army had been his only dream for most of his life. The rejection tipped him over that fine edge of sanity that we all walked so carefully. He needed to find something else to believe in, including himself.

He never did.

We heard that he had jumped from The Gap. A windswept cliff face that has lured folks to a watery grave for many, many years.

We cried.

I am crying now. Dear God what a waste of precious people.

It is so damned hard writing about them now. There are no cemeteries where I can go to lay flowers. No shrine to their talents, their dreams and their lives.

Just the memories of who they were, and what gifts they gave me by allowing me to share in their lives for such a short time.

I will not forget.

Jenny was just beautiful, fragile and delicate. She had met a guy when she turned sixteen and had been living with him for several years. Jamie and I were concerned though, she didn't talk about her life at all; she was content to ask all the questions, but not answer any herself.

We all exchanged phone numbers and promised to ring each other if we ever needed help of any kind.

We had decided back in year one of our meetings to never allow our early lives to intrude on our current ones. It was a pact we made. My life with these amazing people was something I treasured, and held dear to my heart.

It seemed a betrayal to me that I couldn't share how important they were to me. Yet I had been in full agreement with the decision we had made. We now each had lives unconnected with our pasts. These new lives and identities were our present and our future. The past was an unwelcome intrusion. We wouldn't allow the things that had happened to us dirty up our current world.

Jamie was very much a man now. All traces of the younger version had disappeared, except for his uncanny knack of reading me like a book.

He had a home, and a live in girlfriend. I was so pleased he appeared to be happy with his life.

Chapter 24

Jeff and I had been married for seven years. They were happy times. For the most part Jeff seemed content with life; although I know, the hospitals and late night dashes to emergency took their toll on him.

We continued our physical relationship; I felt such guilt at not being able to respond the way I felt I should. He didn't complain, for the moment I was able to satisfy him; we never talked about it.

His treatment of me didn't alter. He remained calm, in control and loving.

I had been spiraling further into depression in the years since having the ectopic pregnancy.

The doctors were right. I couldn't carry a baby. Two further miscarriages had proven that.

I accepted finally that children were something that wouldn't be part of my life.

Jeff had accepted it from the day we were told.

Jeff's contract was up and he was offered another three-year extension. We decided to leave. It was time.

Coming home was just so good, even though we had flown back for Christmas each year it wasn't the same.

Jeff's mom and dad had been to visit us in New Guinea a couple of times, but there was nothing like coming home again.

It was such a difficult thing for dad to do. He had fought the Japanese up on the Kokoda trail and had sworn he would never set foot in the country again.

But we were his family, and accordingly he put his dreadful memories of the place to one side.

We'd been back from New Guinea about 8 weeks or so I guess, having accepted another post in Northern Queensland. I started to feel ill. No pain this time, just a great deal of vomiting and an aversion to food.

The food part was the strangest. Since the days on the streets when I often had nothing to eat, food had become important to me on a big scale.

Jeff thought I had picked up something overseas, a bug of some sort. So I went to the doctor.

He took some blood and said to drink fluids and rest. He'd have the results back the next day.

The doctor's surgery phoned around midday the following day.

My results were back and the doctor wanted to see both Jeff and myself. They gave me an appointment for late that afternoon.

I phoned Jeff and he arrived at the doctors in time for our appointment.

The doctor was a lovely man. We were called in and took our seats. Both of us trying to guess what the doctor would say. I wasn't a panic merchant; but must admit I was concerned that we had both been called in.

He glanced down at the paperwork and then looked at me. "Stacey my dear, you are pregnant. About 10 week's along." he said.

"Ten weeks!" I felt a rush of joy. I had never managed to carry beyond the first 4 weeks. I touched my abdomen gently.

"Is it all right...the baby, I mean it's not in the other tube or anything is it?"

"I'll do further tests, my dear. What I want to say to both of you is this; if the pregnancy is viable then in order for you to carry to term I would want you hospitalized."

Jeff had been quiet, but he was holding my hand so tight it hurt, "Hospital? She's spent too much time in hospitals already. She can rest at home, can't she?"

"In my opinion she would be better off in hospital, at least for the first and maybe the second trimester. You both may never get another opportunity like this. I have found that women seldom actually rest at home when ordered to. For the moment let's verify the baby's viability, shall we. Once that is clear, the decision can be made."

"How is it that I am still having a period, doctor?"

"Is the period normal, for you I mean, Stacey?"

"It's not nearly as heavy as I'm used to."

"It's not unheard of for a woman to continue to menstruate during pregnancy; I will refer you to a specialist and have him do the tests."

The doctor wrote a covering letter to a Gynecologist in the local area. I wanted this baby so very much. I was scared to death that this little one wouldn't be in the womb properly. I was excited that I was already ten weeks along...I had miscarried well before this twice before.

Jeff had very little to say on the way home; although we did decide not to tell his parents or our friends about the baby until the specialist confirmed that the pregnancy was viable.

The Gynecologist's office confirmed my appointment and Jeff went along with me. Neither of us talked much about the pregnancy, it was understood that we may be in for bad news.

The Gynecologist had ultrasound equipment in his suite of rooms.

I wanted to ask the radiologist what she could see as she ran the probe over my abdomen. The gel was cold… I tried to focus on the ceiling …the walls anywhere at all, but I couldn't take my eyes of her face. Surely, she would give something away.

She hadn't. She simply wiped the remaining gel off my stomach and asked me to get dressed and return to the waiting room.

Jeff and I sat quietly holding hands and waiting.

We had been waiting for around 40 minutes I think when we were summoned back into the doctor office.

We sat…each gripping the others hand tightly. My thoughts were utterly chaotic, and Jeff was being stoic as always.

"Well now…Congratulations to you both. Your pregnancy is viable. The ultrasound indicates that you are approximately 12 weeks pregnant.

"Your doctor has indicated that you have had several miscarriages my dear. He feels and I agree that hospitalizing you for complete bed rest would be the best way to proceed."

Jeff and I were so busy hugging each other and crying we barely heard the man.

"Can't she rest at home?" asked Jeff hopefully.

"In my experience it's best that my patients who have conceived but failed to carry are best hospitalized to give the baby the maximum chance of being delivered full term.

"Perhaps we can allow your wife weekend leave. It will depend on how well the pregnancy is progressing.

"Can my husband and I discuss the hospital option and contact you tomorrow?" I asked in a voice I scarcely recognized. My happiness and fear were warring inside me for dominance. Happiness was winning so far.

"Of course. Once you have reached a decision we can make appropriate arrangements. Please don't prolong the decision. I feel it is necessary to have you in a room and resting as soon as possible.

We shook his hand and left. I don't think our feet actually touched the sidewalk. Jeff gave me a huge hug. "I love you, Stacey. Don't forget that."

I sniffled back the tears and clung to his hand.

We decided to telephone Mom and Dad after dinner.

Their excitement almost equaled ours.

There really was no choice in my mind; I would do everything in my power to ensure our little one survived. If that meant long hospitalization then so be it.

My darling mother-in-law understood completely, the men didn't seem so certain.

Ultimately, it was left for me to decide. I chose the hospital.

I was admitted two days later. The nurses were so marvelous, once a day I was helped into a wheelchair and taken out into the lovely rose gardens for fresh air. I was in a private room at Jeff's insistence. Jeff came every night. We sat and watched television together not talking much. We had discussed buying our first home before I found out about the baby. This posting was meant to be a permanent one, so we had looked and happily found a place we could afford.

I had been in hospital for a month and everything was progressing well. Apart from my intense boredom, which was really so insignificant in the scheme of things. I watched television and had an enormous stack of books to read courtesy of the staff, and Jeff.

The late shift of nurses would pop in and play card games with me once they had bedded down and settled the other patients. The sound of crying babies filtered into my room often. I would stroke my stomach and chat to the baby, telling her I was excited about her, and promising her that her world would be a special magical place. I would make it that way.

Something deep inside told me I was having a girl. But it didn't matter; it didn't matter at all.

I was permitted weekend leave at last, and with promises to rest made, Jeff took me home.

My maternal instincts were kicking in hard. But I was also aware that it would take a lot of work setting up our first real home. To date we had lived with the folks or in company provided housing. We had basic furniture but not nearly enough to furnish a three bedroom home. I wanted a nursery for our baby. A special place…warm and safe.

We had such a wonderful time picking things out and furnishing the nursery. It was fresh, new, and lovely.

Our baby was due late February. I developed toxemia and the weekend leave was stopped as a precaution. I could no longer see my toes, amongst other things.

February came and went and the baby seemed to be in no hurry to leave her warm safe place.

The doctor decided to induce me.

Jeff and I were nervous, excited, happy…and scared.

I went into labor immediately after the induction…I remained in labor for 29 hours with Jeff at my side for the entire time. It was a difficult birth. The doctor wanted to do a caesarian when we went into hour 30. I was exhausted. The baby was not showing any signs of distress however.

I asked if we had another option, and the doctor said yes, he could do an episiotomy and deliver our little one that way, but he was concerned that I had already been worn down with the long labor.

I had not spent all these months in hospital to be asleep when our baby was born. It would in all probability be the only time I could have a baby, and as long as she was showing no signs of distress, I wanted to be aware of every moment of her arrival.

The doctor gave me several strong local injections and then he delivered our beautiful precious baby girl. I have never before or since experienced a rush of love and joy like it.

Our daughter weighed in at lb. 12ozs. She was 22 inches long…and had a great set of lungs and a mass of dark hair.

For the very first time in my life, I was grateful to have been born a woman.

Jeff cried openly when she was placed in his arms.

I gazed down at her and checked her toes, fingers and everything else. How did we create something so beautiful?

That feeling has never left me.

We named her Althea. It was the beginning of the happiest days of my life. The memories of all those days linger even now.

Jeff was a good father. He was so gentle with her.

As for me…I spent my time ensuring that her world was safe, and made it as magical and special as I could.

She would never know hunger. She would never doubt for one moment that her life was special or that she was unconditionally loved.

Her proud Grandparents doted on her.

She grew into a mischievous pixie of a child, she was always going to be tall and I did my best to ensure that she walked tall and proud in her world.

A world that was filled with people who loved her. She had all the birthdays and Easter egg hunts, all the Christmas surprises under the tree. She had friends over all the time, the house seemed perpetually filled with laughter; we took her best friend on holidays with us so that she would never be a lonely only child.

It simply isn't possible to describe how happy I was during those years.

Chapter 25

My health was bad. Very bad. It was deteriorating fast. I was hospitalized often, and Jeff was working and unable to cope with our daughter on his own. His mom began coming over and staying in our home whenever I was hospitalized to be certain the little one was well cared for during my lengthy stays. And to help Jeff cope.

Jeff would bring Althea in of a morning briefly to see me, and again during the evening hours. Our daughter became accustomed to seeing her mommy connected to tubes. That worried me so very much. I felt enormous guilt as if somehow I was letting both of them down. Jeff hadn't signed on for this.

The stuff about "In sickness and in health" didn't mean no married life to speak of…

I often left it too late before giving in and going to hospital. Hoping against hope that the pain would stop of its own volition. It didn't and my delaying matters only made it worse.

Over the years, I was hospitalized over 56 times. In most cases for longer than a week at a stretch. I had had eight major operations trying to correct the long-term damage to my pancreas.

We searched everywhere for a doctor that would be prepared to take me on as a patient, outside of the hospital environment.

We found one.

This doctor gave us some different choices. He was prepared to treat me at home if the pain struck during his office hours. He wrote prescriptions for heavy-duty narcotic relief (Morphine) that Jeff would administer by injection into the muscles of my behind.

That was the beginning of the years I was to spend in a Morphine induced fog.

I lost track of where the pain left of and the addiction to the morphine kicked in.

Apparently, no one outside could see it. I appear to have responded to the world on autopilot, with only our daughter and Jeff seeing through my shield of normality.

Life continued and the years sped by.

Jeff never spoke of being unhappy. He would do anything and everything to avoid an emotional scene. I had never heard him raise his voice in anger. We had never ever had a fight.

I regret that more than I can say. At least if we had been fighting I may have been aware that we had big problems within the marriage.

As it was the cost of my medication was crippling. Jeff was under enormous strain. I went back to work to try and help. I lost count of the number of times I lost my jobs due to lengthy stays in hospital.

I was still living in a fool's paradise the day that Jeff asked for a divorce.

We had been married 27 years.

My entire world imploded.

I am getting teary just thinking about it now. All the if only's in the world won't make it go away.

He was in love with someone else.

There was no discussion, no marriage counseling. No screaming and crying.

In one sharp slice, it was over…and he was gone.

Twelve months later the divorce was granted. Our lovely home went on the market. Our daughter moved in with her father and his girlfriend as I had nowhere for her and I to go.

We had taken out a second mortgage to build an extension on the house; the purchase price barely covered it.

I was franticly searching for a place I could afford to rent on a disability support pension.

I was utterly terrified that after 27 years I would end up back on the streets.

The family that I cherished was ripped apart.

My darling in-laws were shattered, but of course, they had to be supportive of Jeff and his new lady.

They knew what a toll my health and its consequences had taken, but never in their worst nightmares did they expect us to get divorced.

I applied for public housing.

I was allocated a tiny bedsit in an outer suburb of Sydney. I didn't care about how small or badly treated it was. It was a room. I had a roof over my head. That's all that mattered.

I was hospitalized for 8 weeks soon after moving in to the bedsit. I didn't see my daughter once during that time. She was a teenager, living through something that had shattered her safe world. Our relationship was strained, she wanted to be with me, but at that stage in her short life, hospitals and my being ill was a constant reminder of the fact that her family had shattered.

She didn't blame anyone for what had happened. She had known her father wasn't very happy.

I made the decision during that long spell in hospital to stop using prescribed morphine. I needed to have all my wits about me, and I wanted to know just where the damned pain stopped and the need for the morphine began.

I went cold turkey while in hospital care. I have never been a person that could do things in half measures. It was all or nothing and the doctors supported my decision. Providing I remained in hospital till the drug and my need for it were out of my system.

I don't recommend doing cold turkey. It was horrendous.

But I left that hospital clear headed, and wondering bitterly just where all those years had gone.

I continued to have severe attacks of pain. However, I refused morphine if it was offered. Unless the doctors were worried about my blood pressure and my body's ability to cope with the onset of pain. They monitored it closely and only gave me morphine as an absolute last resort to allow me to recover, and to let me recuperate.

I use no pain medication whatsoever at home.

I isolated myself from everyone. Finding that the friends I'd had were embarrassed and didn't want to be seen to be taking sides in a divorce that stunned everyone.

I wasn't the only one who never thought it could happen to us.

That was over twelve years ago.

Chapter 26

I had lived alone only once, the three months on the streets before I went to the palace. The thought of doing it again frightened me.

I had been protected and nurtured for 27 years; the memories of the time before that took on a darker shadow.

I isolated myself deliberately, refusing offers of friendship. I couldn't do that again. I was weary of a world that clearly I wasn't meant to be happy in.

I felt sorry for myself, and all traces of the fight that was once in me seemed to have given up and left.

I started drinking. I would sit alone every night, play my favorite music, and drink myself to sleep.

Soon, I began finding reasons to start drinking earlier and earlier. Until a time came when I would awaken and begin to drink until I passed out. I would wake again and start again.

This went on for four years. I was committing slow suicide.

I woke one morning 5 years ago and clearly recall being disappointed that I had woken up at all. I caught that thought; it shook me to the foundation of my soul.

So many of us had done just that.

Suicide? Was that an option for me?

The answer was no.

Somewhere in the befuddled mess I had made of myself, Sassy still lingered.

Sassy began to fight back…again. Finally.

I booked myself into a detox ward in the local hospital, and as I had done with the morphine, I went cold turkey off the booze.

I haven't had a drink now for 5 years.

My life has taken on a new edge, and I love it.

My relationship with my darling daughter has never been better. So good, in fact that six months ago she suggested that we share rented accommodation together.

We have done just that, and the days and nights have taken on a warmth and security that I have craved for so very long. Yet I had been happy living alone for the past 5 years; I had finally accepted that the lost years could not be re-lived.

I accepted that being alone was just fine, in fact, I loved it.

Mind you, I must admit that this is better. She works full time and I have the days alone...Oh...Except for the cat. I love the days as well. I write constantly now; working on fiction books, which I have found a damned sight easier than this is to write.

The nights are fun. We take turns cooking dinner and enjoy sharing it.

She has a very busy social life and throws herself into everything she does with love and enthusiasm.

We respect each other's privacy completely.

Then we have a couple of Girl nights a month. Munchies and a movie, or a live concert and dinner in town.

I am having the most marvelous time.

My daughter has grown now and she remains the constant light in my life. I cannot hope to express the pride she makes me feel. I am so privileged to be a part of her life. I have watched her grow into a physically beautiful woman. More importantly, I have had the pleasure of watching her evolve into a warm, loving, feisty and delightful human being.

From a very early age, I watched her as she came to understand her world. I watched her fight for the rights of her friends. I watched her champion those unable to stand and fight for themselves. I watched as she took the lumps, bumps, and sometimes the bruises associated with being a true friend. I watched her love and I watched her suffer loss. She and I have shared, and continue to share, some wonderful moments, those sparkling champagne moments that linger in the memory and bring a smile to me long after they have occurred.

She lives every moment of her life. There are no spaces in her world for people who are cruel, unkind or prejudiced in any way. She loves with all of herself, throwing caution to the wind and sticking her chin out at the world.

She cries with sadness and she cries with laughter; half measures will never be a part of her life. She simply doesn't have any idea how to give less than all she is to the people she believes in.

I am honored to call her my daughter and privileged to call her my friend.

The Honor Roll

The people in the list below were all dear to me. They were my friends. They were not perfect angels, not the movers and shakers of this strange old world, but they were good people. I wouldn't even attempt to portray them as anything other than flawed and damaged human beings.

They gave of themselves and contributed more to my life than I can ever hope to express. The people on the list below are dead now. They have died in most cases by their own hand. Illness and advanced age took only two of them. I have listed them in no particular order. They were all equally important

The Fly man - jumped to his death from a cliff.

Tilly - took her own life with sleeping tablets and alcohol.

Animal - was killed in a clash with a rival biker gang.

Carol - died of AIDS-related pneumonia.

Kirsty - died of cancer

John - overdosed on heroin.

Alison - died of carbon monoxide poisoning.

Elizabeth (Momma) - died of AIDS-related pneumonia.

Lexie - died in prison.

Pete - died in a car accident whilst under the influence of alcohol

Dulcie - died of natural causes, aged 86.

Eunice - passed away in her sleep, aged 89.

On Tuesday September 1 2008, Baby Jenny committed suicide at age 49. The reasons why, I still can't touch.

Epilogue

December 1 is just two days away. Jamie and I have been in touch and we will meet, as always, outside the Opera House at noon. We will laugh and we will cry. Most of all we will talk about the future and how exciting it will be. We will not say goodbye. Those that we loved aren't gone, they live on in our memories and they will do that for as long as we draw breath. I will forever see them in my mind and in the places of my youth, and I will smile when I hear those faint echoes of laughter.

Thank you for allowing me to share these moments of my life with you.

A note from the author.

Thank you all. If you would care to learn more about my life, I will be releasing my latest book in this series by October 2016.

"Still Sassy at Sixty" picks up, where this book left off.